Encyclopedia of LEGLOCKS
Brazilian Jiu Jitsu

by Rigan Machado

EMPIRE Books
P.O. Box 491788, Los Angeles, CA 90049

Disclaimer

Please note that the author and publisher of this book are NOT RESPONSIBLE in any manner whatsoever for any injury that may result from practicing the techniques and/or following the instructions given within. Since the physical activities described herein may be too strenuous in nature for some readers to engage in safely, it is essential that a physician be consulted prior to training.

Published in 2006 by Empire Books.
Copyright © 2006 by Empire Books.

All rights reserved. No part of this publication may be reproduced or utilized in any form or by any means, electronic or mechanical, including photocopying, recording, or by any information storage and retrieval system, without prior written permission from Empire Books.

Library of Congress Cataloging-in-Publication Data

ISBN-10: 1-933901-14-4
ISBN-13: 978-1-933901-14-5

Machado, Rigan.
  Encyclopedia of leglocks / Rigan Machado. -- 1st ed.
     p. cm.
  Includes index.
  ISBN 1-933901-14-4 (pbk. : alk. paper)
 1. Jiu-jitsu--Brazil. I. Title.
  GV1114.M3393 2006
  796.815'20981--dc22
             2006009373
Empire Books
P.O. Box 491788
Los Angeles, CA 90049
(818) 767-7900

First edition
07 06 05 04 03 02 01 00 99 98 97 1 3 5 7 9 10 8 6 4 2
Printed in the United States of America.

Editor: Bob Magath
Action Photography: Tom Fitzpatrick
Interior Photography: Jason Alan
Interior & Cover Design: Mario M. Rodriguez, MMR Design Solutions

This book is dedicated to Brazilian Jiu Jitsu practitioners around the world.

Introduction ix

Attacks from the Ground 1

Attacks from the Standing Position 143

Conclusion 204

ACKNOWLEDGEMENTS

To Bob Magath, for his time and effort cleaning and polishing the manuscript. Your dedication is truly appreciated.

To Jason Alan, who put in many hours in front of the camera capturing all the technical details of an extensive repertoire of leglocks.

To Tom Fitzpatrick, writer and photographer, who supplied wonderful action and competition photographs.

To Fernando Sabatino, who provided excellent cooperation and skills while demonstrating the painful techniques in this book.

ABOUT THE AUTHOR

RIGAN MACHADO

Rigan Machado is a direct student with lineage tracing back to the art's founder, Carlos Gracie. He is one of the top instructors of Brazilian Jiu Jitsu in the world. His long experience in teaching—to everyone from beginners to world champions—and his contributions to BJJ's teaching methods have brought him worldwide acclaim. Originally from Rio de Janeiro, Brazil, his credits include many of the top Brazilian nationals and international championships. Rigan Machado was one of the first Brazilian black belts moving to the United States, where he became one of the leading forces in expanding the art created by the Gracie family. "Brazil was just the beginning of the grappling movement. But from there, the seeds have been spread all around the world. If a student is not from Brazil and he becomes a world champion, then that makes me a good teacher and makes me happy," says Machado.

Despite his fame, he continues to train with a dedication born out of the love of his art. Rigan also has appeared in several movies and TV series, becoming one of the most recognizable figures in the world of the martial arts. Highly regarded as one of the most talented technicians and teachers ever to come out of the Gracie family, Rigan has been instrumental in the development of the Machado Jiu Jitsu, as it is known today. *"Finding a harmony between mind and body is the ultimate goal of any martial artist, but the physical techniques must come first. A calm and concentrated awareness is the key toward the realization of personal potential, of which technical mastery is the first step,"* says Machado. Drawing on his considerable knowledge, Rigan Machado has published extensively and authored several DVD series on Brazilian Jiu Jitsu under the tutelage of EM3 VIDEO.

INTRODUCTION

Due to the recent increase in the number of Brazilian Jiu Jitsu (BJJ), Submission Grappling, and Mixed Martial Art (MMA) enthusiasts, the need for a book about leg-locks has become imperative. It is with this need in mind that the present work is offered.

In Brazilian Jiu Jitsu and Submission Grappling, the legs always come into play due to the use of one of the most revolutionary techniques in the last two decades—the guard. The different types of guard (close, open, spider, butterfly, etc.) are a very favorable situation to apply not only sweeps, reversal, and chokes but also to defeat the opponent with all kinds of leg-locks.

Submission fighters, MMA fighters and BJJ fighters today all have leg-locks in their arsenal as part of their attacking tools. And there is a reason why—this submission technique is almost always a surprise and can change the course of a fight in two seconds flat.

Defeating an opponent by submission has never been an easy task, but when you try to do it using a leg-lock, the chances of getting a clean submission are dramatically reduced. This is due to the fact that trying to get a hold on a strong limb like a leg is not easy. Not only does your grip on his leg and hips have to be perfectly adjusted, but your own hip position also has to be altered to better fit the technique.

The legs are one of the most vulnerable parts of the body…if attacked properly. In order to do that you have to learn how the joints in the legs move. Unfortunately, many fighters neglect to learn this basic anatomy, and when they try to apply a leg-lock technique, it simply doesn't work. The Japanese fighters in the early 1980s and 1990s were notorious for their application of leg submissions from all positions. They were very knowledgeable in hip, knee, Achilles, and heel-twisting locks. In the mid-to-late 1990s, the practitioners of Brazilian Jiu Jitsu accepted the use of leg-locks and began employing them in competition (although for many years, leg-locks were seldom used due to the implicit danger to the knees).

INTRODUCTION

Brazilian Jiu Jitsu fighters today all utilize leg-locks as an important part of their attacking arsenal. If they don't use them as a main attacking point, they at least have enough knowledge of leg-locks to utilize them as a finishing move.

For the BJJ student, leg-locks should be taught later on in the tactical game, so the practitioner can develop dexterity with his legs to develop his guard game and to learn the use of the legs in proper order and with correct action. The open guard, utilizing the legs and hooks to attack and defend, is basically the most dangerous and vulnerable position for being caught in an effective leg-lock. For proper control of your opponent's actions, one of your feet will always be placed on the opponent's hips. It is here that your legs are vulnerable.

Every grappler and BJJ fighter who competes today needs to have a working knowledge of the use, defense, and passing of all the various guard positions and how vulnerable these are to being attacked by a devastating leg-lock. It is important that you can identify these guards and train the games of sweeping, bridging, passing, attacking, striking, and defending the strikes utilizing the leg positions from both the top and bottom positions. It is also important to simultaneously learn how to attack the opponent's legs and how to protect yourself from a leg-lock attack.

Don't focus solely on trying to get the submission via a leg-lock, because this tactical approach will make your game one-dimensional and all your actions will become predictable. To be able to submit your opponents via leg-locks, you need to learn how to "disguise" your true intention and how to present a "different" game plan to your opponent.

A fighter is generally strongest when he begins to grapple, so it is important to use other elements in order to wear him down before you attack his legs. While your opponent is preoccupied with escaping from your chokes and arm-locks is when you want to bring all the decisive power of a leg-lock into play. It is easier to catch a lock after your opponent is tired.

Positioning is the key to getting a clean leg-lock. It is very important to develop the ability to identify when the leg is available for you to attack. In order to do that, you must be capable of "reading" your opponent's game from the very beginning. Some fighters are what we call "leg hunters"—they try to catch the leg from the very beginning. This is not a smart thing to do because any attack to the legs implies a serious danger to your neck and your own legs. It is not surprising to see a fighter trying to get a leg-lock end up tapping himself via a fast counter leg-lock from his opponent.

One important element to remember is that because of the nature of the technique itself, and the size and power of the limb that we are attacking [leg], the time required to fully apply a finishing leg-lock is very short. If you get the proper position and grip right away, the time for your opponent to tap will depend on how much pressure you can apply right from the very beginning. It is correct to say that when you "catch" the leg/ankle, you need to get at least 80 percent of the lock from the very beginning. If not, it will be difficult to stop the opponent from escaping your attack.

Some fighters know how to hide their legs well. This doesn't mean they know how to make their legs disappear, but they are experts in keeping their legs in constant motion while maintaining control in the guard position. They are constantly aware of the danger to their legs and as soon as the opponent's hands are close to their legs, they invert the position and simply initiate an attack, putting the opponent into a defensive mode. Remember, when you attack the legs, you need to use two hands for one task, leaving the rest of your body open to attack.

Becoming an expert in getting submission via leg-locks is something that takes time and training. Mat time and lots of drilling is the key to mastering the lethal leg techniques. You have to run through high repetitions of techniques, set-ups, and different attack sequences until you can "feel" the right opportunity without thinking. Sensitivity becomes the necessary attribute. This specific skill will allow you to anticipate the final action and prevent the opponent from getting the right positioning so you can apply the submission. Also, keep your mind free and open so it will be available to attack and see an opportunity as it arises. When you have to think about it, it is already too late.

Anytime you can touch a foot, wrap a leg or under-hook an ankle, you can attack the foot, the knee, or the ankle. Sometimes the size of a guy's leg comes into play when trying to apply an attack to the leg. If an opponent has really big legs, it is harder to knee-bar him. If he has flexible legs, he can make an attempt more difficult.

Some guys also have a high threshold of pain. A compression lock like a hip lock or an Achilles tendon lock, which are based on pain, as opposed to joint compliance locks— where you can actually break something—are not quite as lethal, but they are still quite painful. Making your opponent tap will depend on how much pain he can resist.

INTRODUCTION

DIFFERENT TYPES OF LOCKS

There are different ways to attack the opponent's legs. Each part of the leg offers specific opportunities, and the right technique must be used to be an effective attack. For instance, the technical approach used to apply an ankle-lock won't work if we are trying to get a knee-bar. Therefore, an understanding of the different parts of the leg is mandatory if we want to effectively access the full repertoire of leg-locks.

Knee-bar

The knee-bar is like a huge arm-bar, and hip pressure needs to be fully applied to take advantage of this technique. The key to this lock's effectiveness has to do with the 90-degree angle in the legs, the squeezing of the knees, and the squeezing and hugging of the foot. The control of the heel and the use of the side of the face closest to the ground as a fulcrum, or the closest armpit to your opponent's body, will insure a tight and secure finish. The knee will flex and bend, but will cause severe knee joint, tendon, and ligament damage if put on fully. There are several precautions to be addressed in both the attacker's pressure and the defense to this lethal lock. The effects of this lock can severely damage the entire knee joint, so be knowledgeable, intelligent, and respectful with this leg attack. Sometimes a simple turn in the direction of your foot will open the right angle to nullify a knee-bar attack.

Hip-lock

Hip-locks are unconventional locks that occur once in a while due to a tweak of a leg-lock turned sideways or a technique gone wrong. It is basically the product of an accident. These locks aren't quite so popular because the athletes doing them aren't very knowledgeable in knowing how to apply them. Also, the people to whom they are applied are usually fighters, highly athletic with strong hips which are hard to twist, extend, or contort. Fighters also have the ability to move and not allow

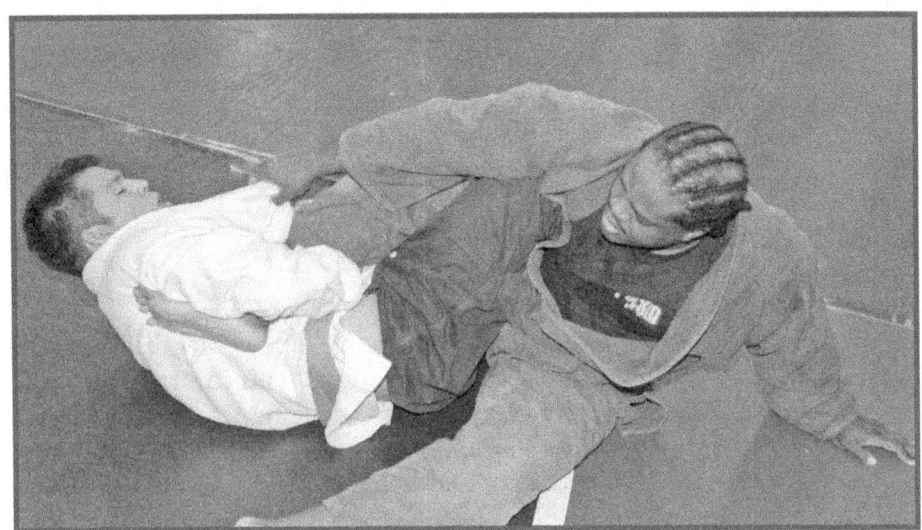

these locks to happen when they feel their body is about to be attacked. Hip-locks are also among the most difficult to apply due to the control points required to make it work.

Heel-hook

The heel-hook is a lock that involves the turning of the ankle and the pulling of the heel. Either the ankle or the knee joint will be affected by this lock. This joint lock is easily accessible and is very dangerous when applied. The pain isn't felt until the ankle or knee dislocates. A high level of care needs to be taken by both the attacker and the defender when this technique is used. The amount of pressure to catch and finish the lock, and the immediate defense as it is applied, are important elements to be practiced during training sessions. Generally, this submission lock is taught to the more advanced submission or professional MMA fighters.

Achilles-lock

This is legal in most BJJ and submission competitions because of its availability and the low level of danger when applied. The only damage that can occur is ligament damage to the ankle. There is no twisting or straightening of any joint except the ankle while being straightened. The Achilles, or ankle lock, is applied by the blade of the forearm and the extension of the hips.

EXECUTION

The anatomical structure of the foot is unique. Unless you understand that, it's hard to destroy the opponent's foot. Applying a foot-lock is

INTRODUCTION

unlike any other submission. There is more than one way to apply pressure and submit an individual. When executing a foot-lock, you can cause temporary pain or permanent damage (which is effective in real-world combat).

The side of the foot has three ligaments and they are not connected to muscle. These ligaments connect bone to bone. They are taut and will not stretch. They essentially hold the foot together. When you squeeze them properly, you can rip those ligaments along the outer portion of the ankle. They are not like the Achilles tendon, which connects bone to muscle along the posterior leg muscles.

The use of the open guard techniques enable the BJJ fighter to sweep his opponent and score points. These guys are very talented with their guard. Some guys have guards that are almost impossible to pass. To counter this technical approach, you have to develop foot-locks from within the guard. You either catch an opponent's foot and he taps, or he worries about it next time because he is now aware of the danger. The idea is to keep the opponent on the run and make him worry. If you don't catch him, it makes him more conservative, which will allow you to play your game. Keep him guessing all the time.

In addition to perfecting foot-locks, it's also important to know all of the escapes from foot-locks. This is the other side of the coin. When you know the escapes, you know where to focus your attention [to prevent your opponent from escaping]. And, of course, when you know the [potential] openings and weaknesses, you can take advantage of these for your own benefit. It's good to know the intricacies of both aspects because you will never get caught by surprise. Don't forget that many of the techniques flow easily into each other. A foot-lock can become an ankle-lock as soon as the opponent turns his knee to the inside of his body. Study different combinations and lock-flows in a fixed pattern. This will allow you to recognize the right technique when the opportunity arises.

Tips

- It is always best to use as much technique and leverage as possible. Strength is used in the end to finish the technique.
- In order for a leg lock to work, you must have the correct leverage points in place.†
- Always try to execute a clean technique and keep your feet hidden.
- Not all techniques apply to all parts of the leg. Study which techniques fit better to specific parts, such as the hip, knee, ankle, and toes.
- Don't stare. You do not want to give away a victory. This means that you want to get so good that you don't give away your move before you actually execute it. Therefore, don't look at his foot before you execute the move. If you stare at the foot, he's going to know what your intentions are. Many BJJ competitors make this simple mistake. Never look at your target. Feel it, don't look at it.
- Big legs are harder to knee-bar because of the strength in the muscles, ligaments and tendons of the leg and knee. Flexibility and strong legs result in the same thing.
- When executing a leg-lock, use the middle of your forearm because power comes from the radial bone, which is about an inch down from your hand. Use the "V," or the area between your biceps and forearm to separate the foot from the leg.
- Try to properly adapt your body and hip position to get the correct leverage to apply the leg-lock.
- When applying your foot-lock, always be aware of the position of your own feet. You don't want your opponent to catch you in a foot-lock.
- Do not touch your opponent's foot before the application. If you do, you will remind him that foot-locks exist and he will move that foot away from you immediately.
- The objective is to get so good at leg-locks that you don't even attempt them unless you know you're going to get one. You should get to the point that you know it's a done deal when you go for one. When you have that confidence, you won't go for them prematurely. Thus, your opponent cannot anticipate your move.
- Deception is the key, but you have to learn to set your game plan first and know how to disguise your true intentions.
- Don't be one-dimensional and stubborn. You cannot pass up opportunities because you are waiting for the opening you want. Be flexible. You simply have to "complete the other half of the movement your opponent gives you." Don't force a technique, allow it to happen.

XV

ATTACKS FROM THE GROUND

Technique 1	2	Technique 27	74
Technique 2	6	Technique 28	78
Technique 3	10	Technique 29	80
Technique 4	14	Technique 30	82
Technique 5	16	Technique 31	84
Technique 6	18	Technique 32	88
Technique 7	20	Technique 33	92
Technique 8	24	Technique 34	96
Technique 9	28	Technique 35	98
Technique 10	32	Technique 36	102
Technique 11	34	Technique 37	104
Technique 12	36	Technique 38	108
Technique 13	38	Technique 39	110
Technique 14	40	Technique 40	112
Technique 15	42	Technique 41	114
Technique 16	46	Technique 42	116
Technique 17	50	Technique 43	118
Technique 18	52	Technique 44	120
Technique 19	56	Technique 45	122
Technique 20	60	Technique 46	124
Technique 21	62	Technique 47	126
Technique 22	64	Technique 48	128
Technique 23	66	Technique 49	130
Technique 24	68	Technique 50	132
Technique 25	70	Technique 51	136
Technique 26	72	Technique 52	138

ATTACKS FROM THE GROUND

1

2

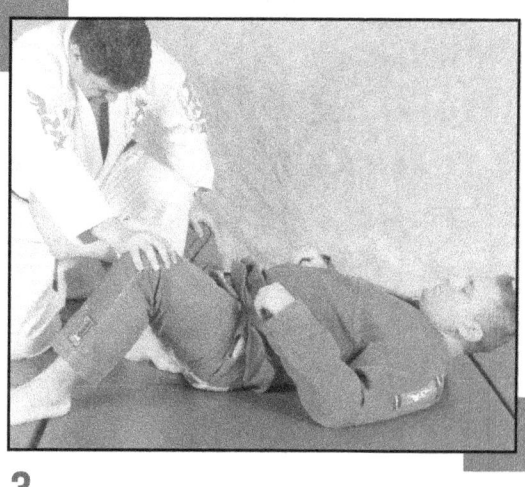
3

Rigan Machado faces his opponent (1). He uses his right hand to open the opponent's left leg (2), and brings his left leg inside the opponent's open guard (3).

TECHNIQUE 1

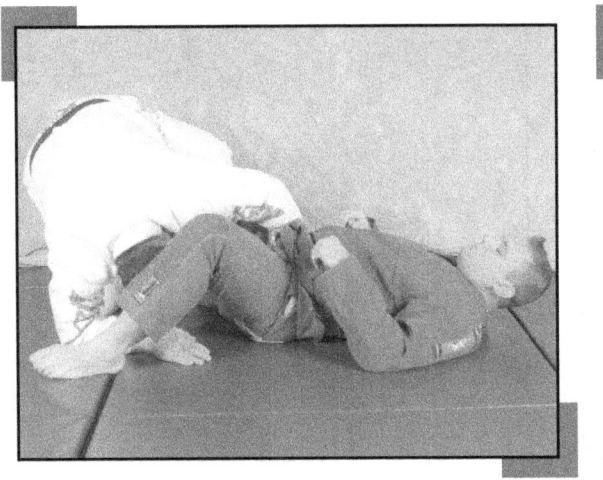
4

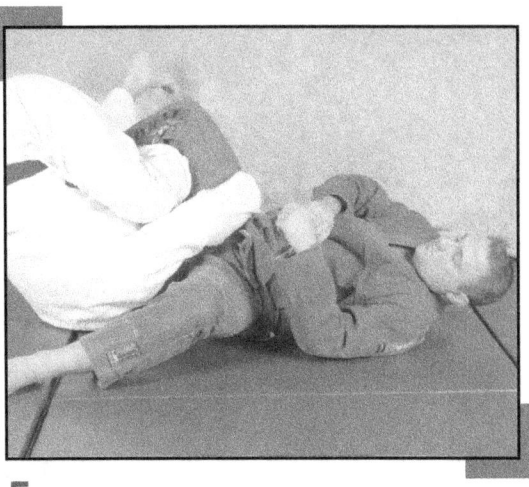
5

Then he starts rolling forward inside the opponent's guard (4), and hooks the opponent's right leg with his right foot (5). Rigan continues rolling forward as he secures the opponent's right thigh with his right hand (6).

6

(continued on next page)

ATTACKS FROM THE GROUND

(continued from previous page)

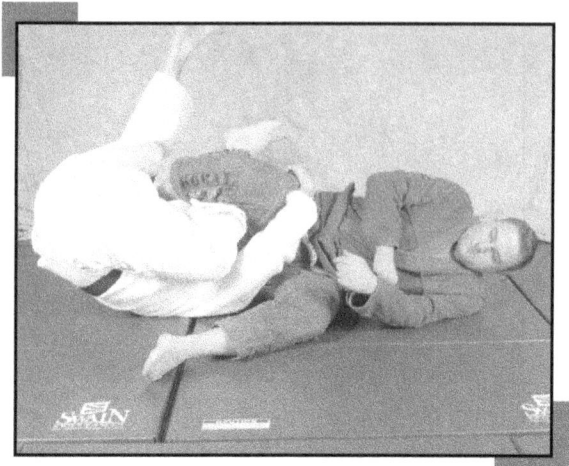
7

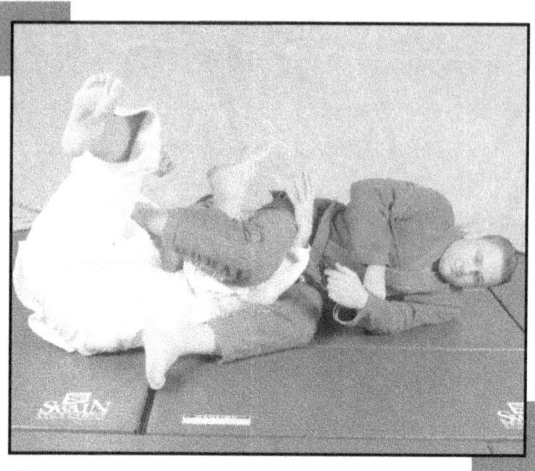
8

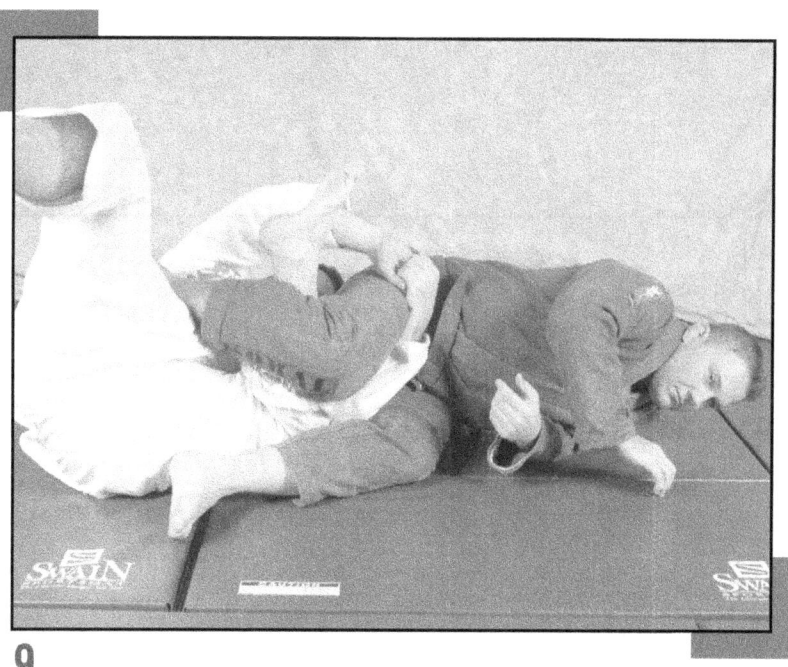
9

TECHNIQUE 1

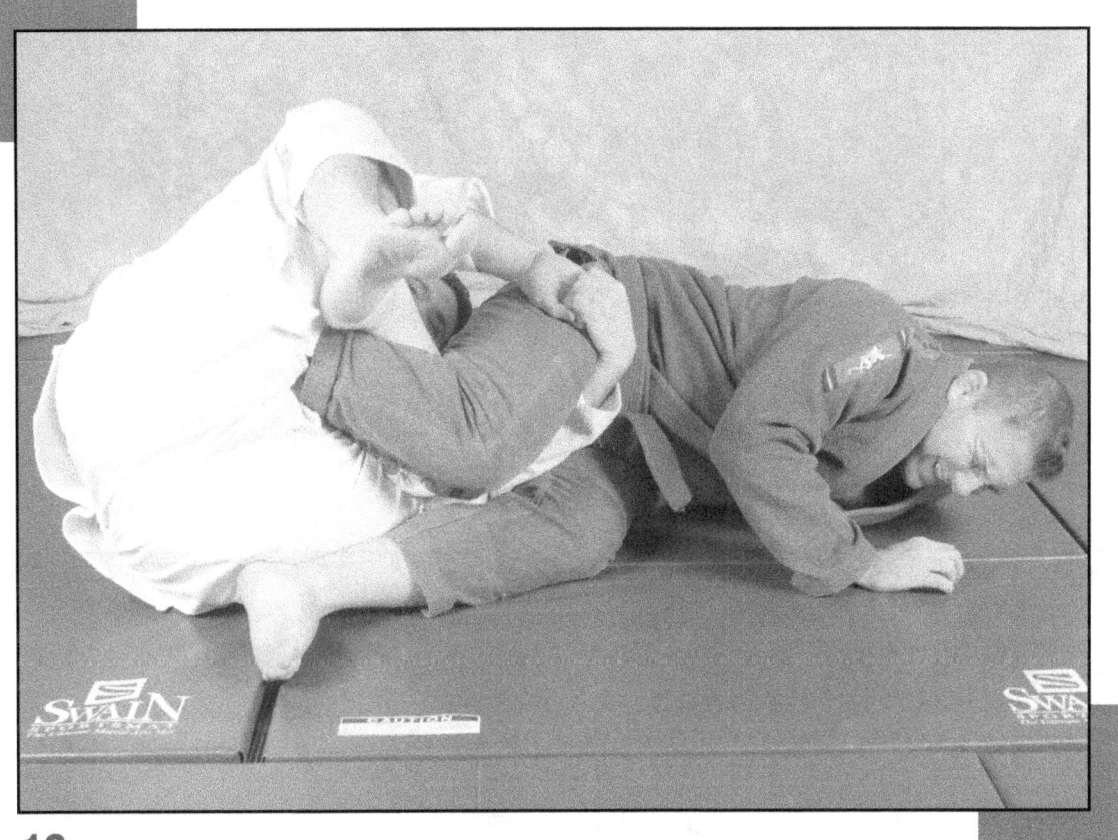
10

He begins to land on his back without losing control of the opponent's body (7). Then, he reaches out with his left hand (8), and grabs his right hand (9). Rigan squeezes hard, and by pressing with his right hip and using his left foot for leverage, he applies a painful leglock to the opponent's right knee (10).

ATTACKS FROM THE GROUND

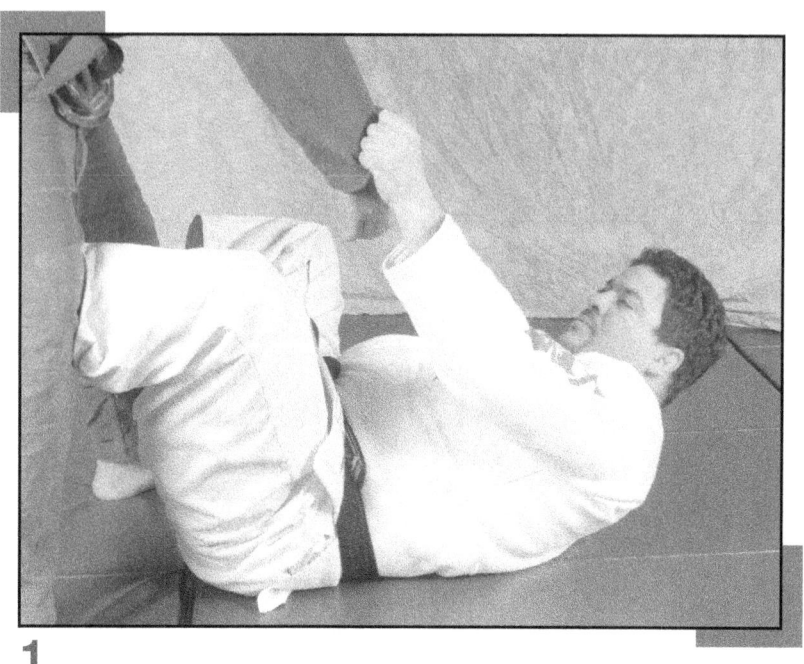

1

2

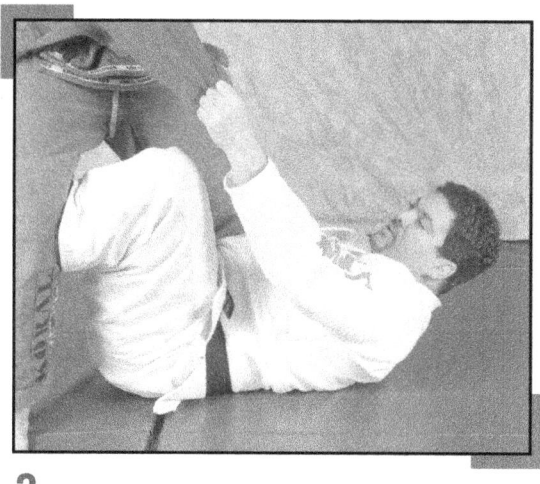

3

Rigan is facing his opponent from the ground (1). He pulls hard on the opponent's right sleeve (2), as he simultaneously uses the hooks to open the opponent's position (3).

TECHNIQUE 2

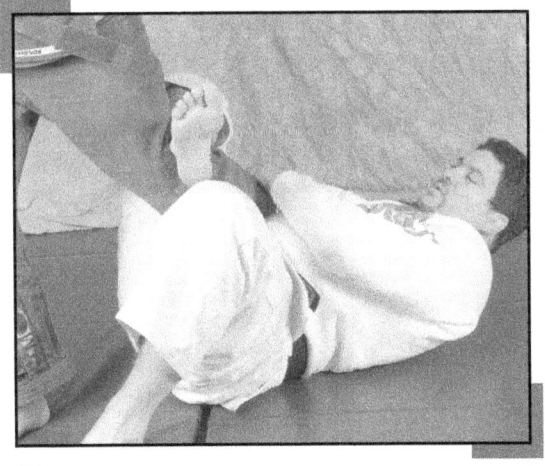
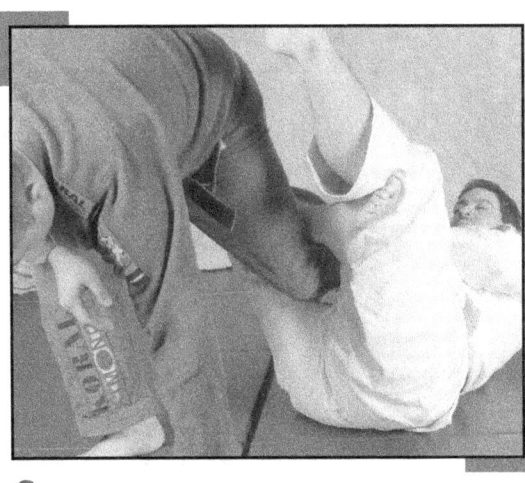

Then, he brings his right leg over the opponent's left leg (4) and presses downward to bring the opponent out of balance (5). Immediately, Rigan passes his left leg over his right instep (6).

(continued on next page)

ATTACKS FROM THE GROUND

(continued from previous page)

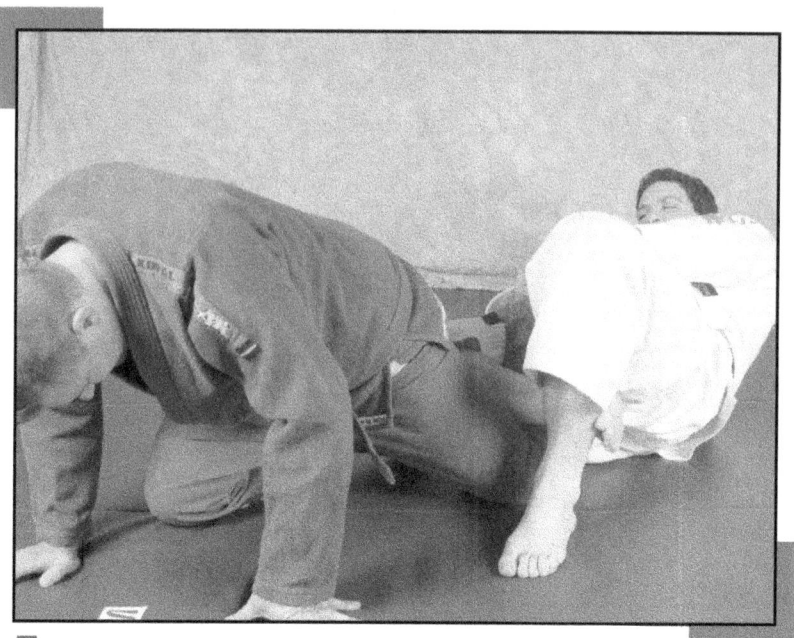
7

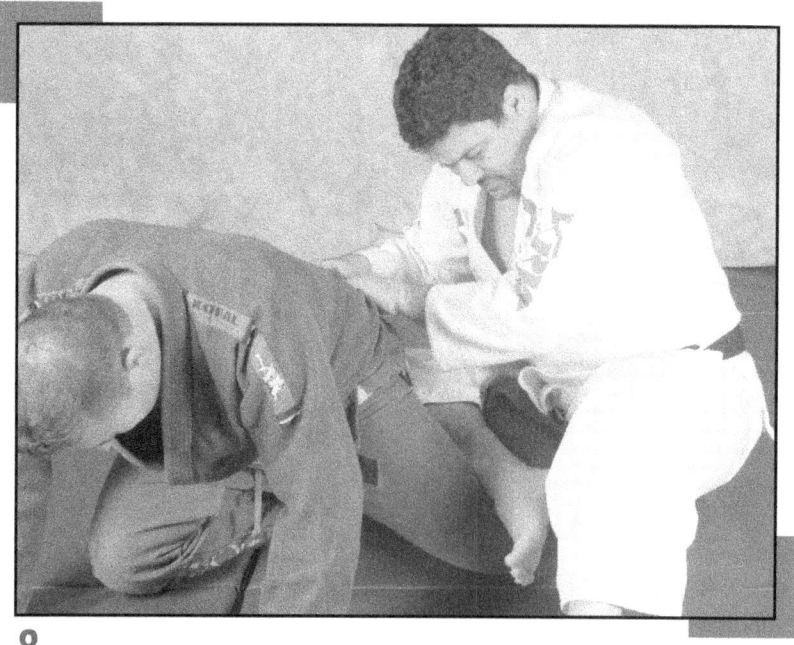
8

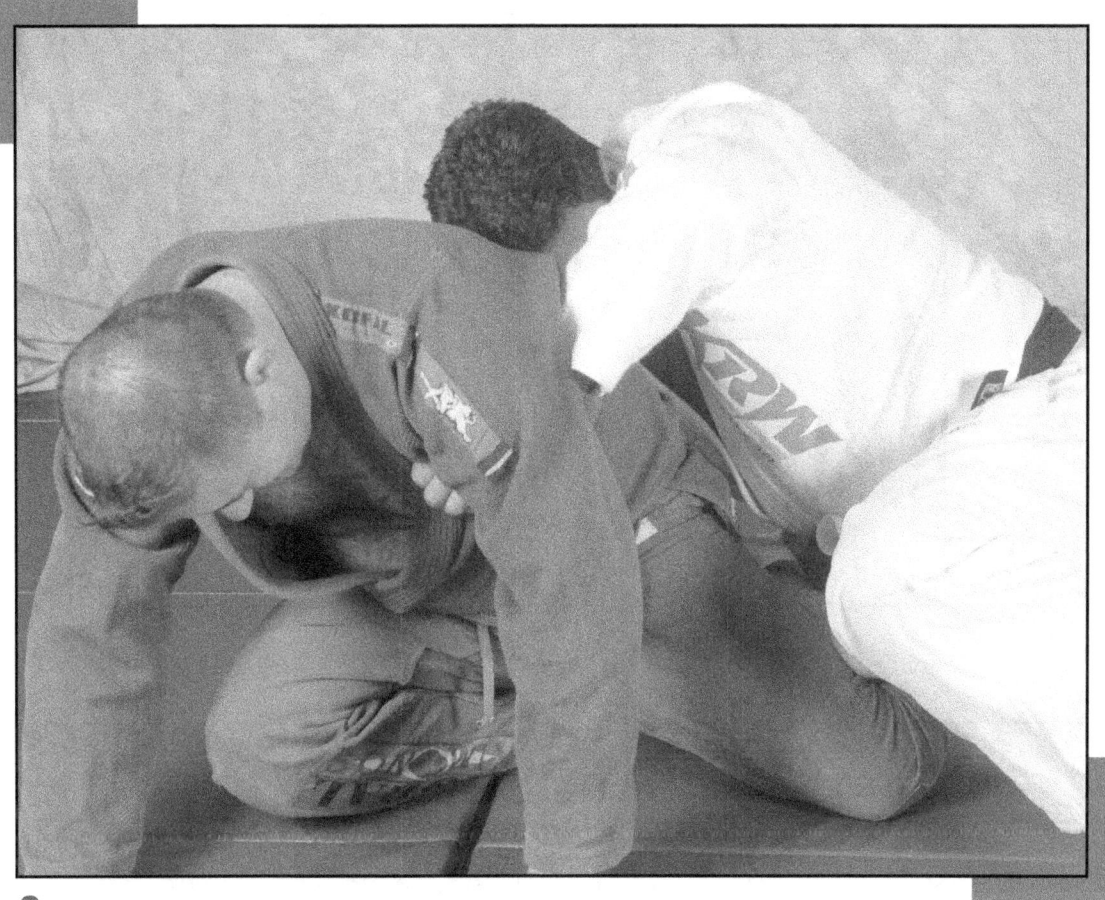

9

He applies pressure to bring the opponent to the ground (7), then he begins to stand up slowly (8) to finalize with a kneelock by bringing his body forward and putting pressure on the opponent's left knee (9).

ATTACKS FROM THE GROUND

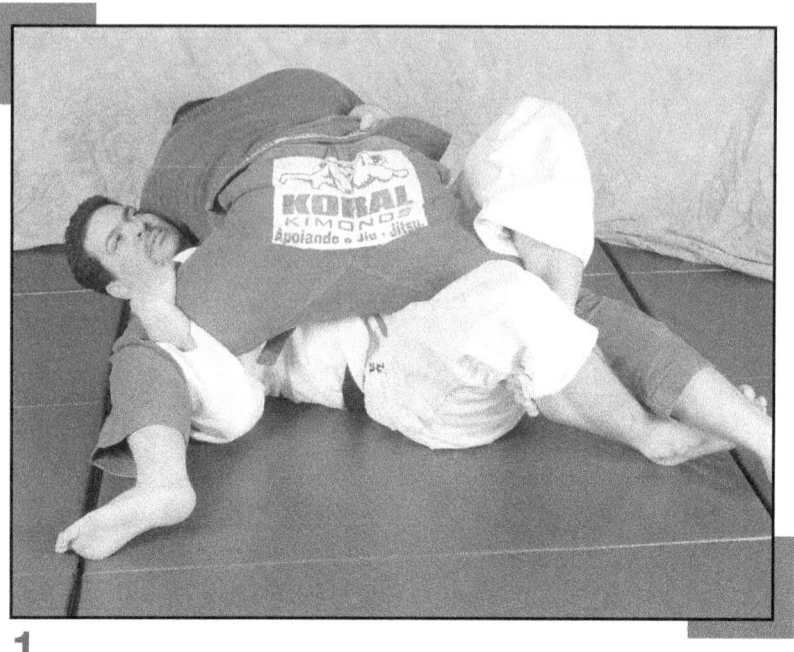

1

2

3

Rigan has control over the opponent inside the half guard (1). By using his right hand and left foot, Rigan begins to lift the opponent's body as he opens space (2) to bring his right leg under the opponent's left leg (3).

Encyclopedia of Leglocks

TECHNIQUE 3

4

5

6

He uses his right thigh to bring the opponent's left foot closer (4), and then traps it between his legs (5). Once this position is secured, Rigan moves the opponent's body to the left side (6).

(continued on next page)

ATTACKS FROM THE GROUND

(continued from previous page)

7

8

9

Now, he begins to move his body forward (7) to push the opponent to the side (8) so he can bring his body weight on top of the opponent and apply a devastating lock to the right knee (9).

ATTACKS FROM THE GROUND

1

2

3

4

Rigan is inside of his opponent's half guard (1). The opponent tries to lock Rigan's right leg and prevent him from passing the guard (2). Rigan slides his body to the side and begins to push the opponent's left knee away from him to create space (3) so he can bring his right hand under the opponent's left knee (4).

TECHNIQUE 4

5

6

7

Rigan grabs his own left hand and secures the grip (5). Then, he leans forward and begins to bring his right foot back (6) to finally hook it behind his own left knee; then, by applying pressure, he gets the opponent into a painful knee-shin lock (7).

ATTACKS FROM THE GROUND

1

2

3

Rigan begins the attack from the opponent's back (1). He brings his body down (2) and passes his right leg between the legs of the opponent, who happens to be on his four (3).

TECHNIQUE 5

4

5

6

Rigan reaches with his left hand and grabs his own right foot (4). Then, he secures the position with the left hand (5) and, by pulling back with both hands and securing his right foot under the back of his left knee, he applies a lock to the opponent's left knee (6).

ATTACKS FROM THE GROUND

Rigan is on the side control with the opponent on his left side (1). The opponent starts to roll to the right side and Rigan takes advantage of the push by using his right hand to bring the left side of the opponent closer to him (2). Then, he brings his right leg up (3) and hooks the opponent's left leg, as he maintains a tight control by grabbing the opponent's belt on the back (4).

1

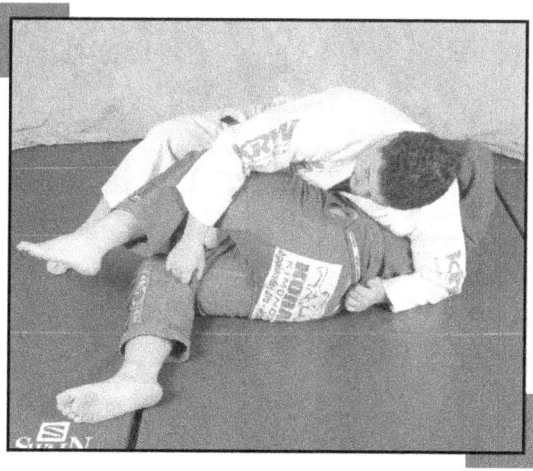
2

3

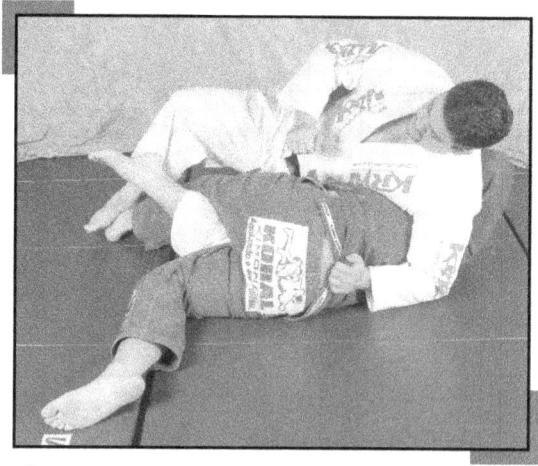
4

TECHNIQUE 6

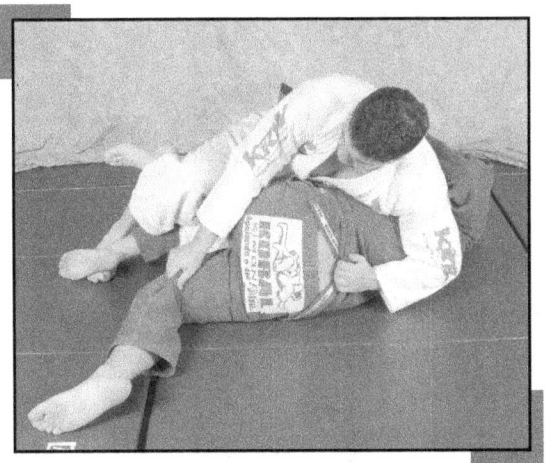
5

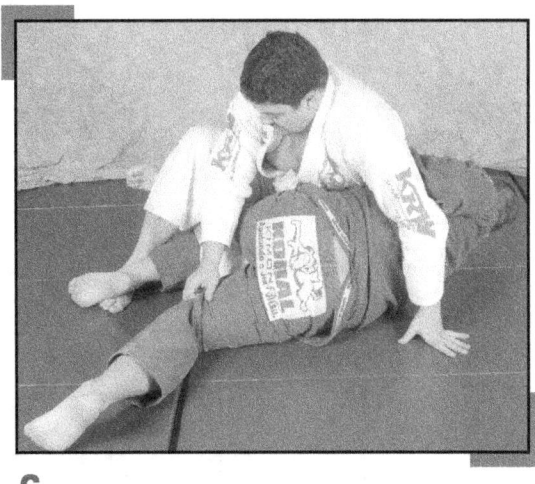
6

7

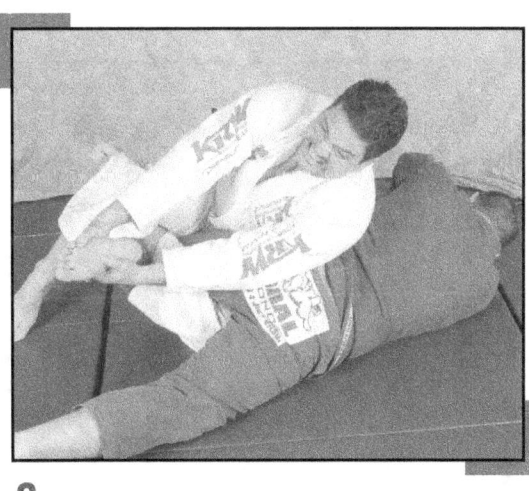
8

Now, Rigan secures the opponent's right leg by grabbing it with his right hand (5). Then he moves his body forward as he uses his left arm to support his body (6), and reaches with his right and left hands for the opponent's left foot (7). Rigan applies a kneelock by pulling the opponent's left foot backward as he keeps his left leg hooked to his right leg to create leverage for the painful lock (8).

ATTACKS FROM THE GROUND

1

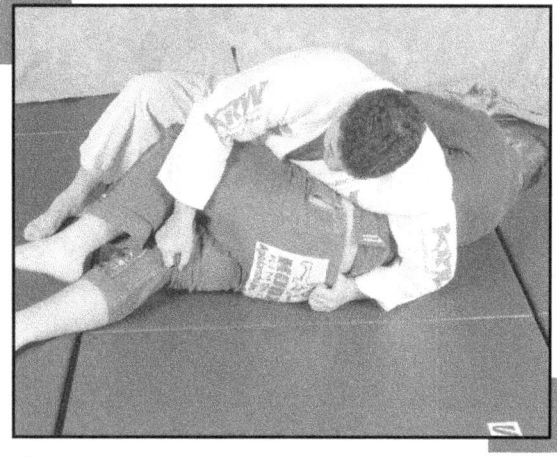

2

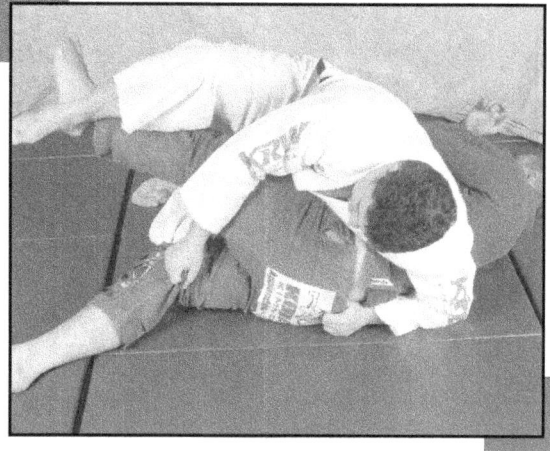

3

Rigan is on the side control with the opponent on his left side (1). The opponent starts to roll to the right side and Rigan takes advantage of the push by using his right hand to bring the left side of the opponent closer to him (2). Then, he brings his right leg up (3).

TECHNIQUE 7

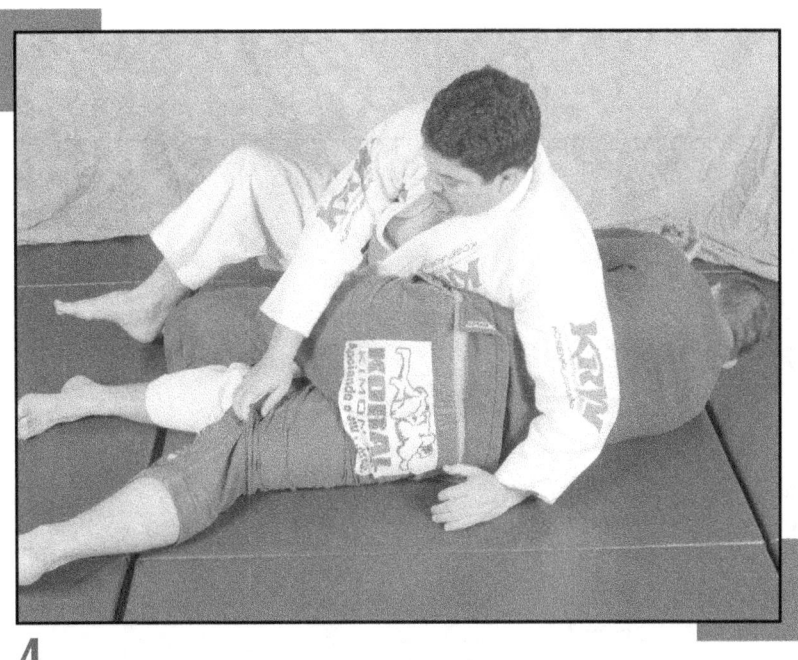

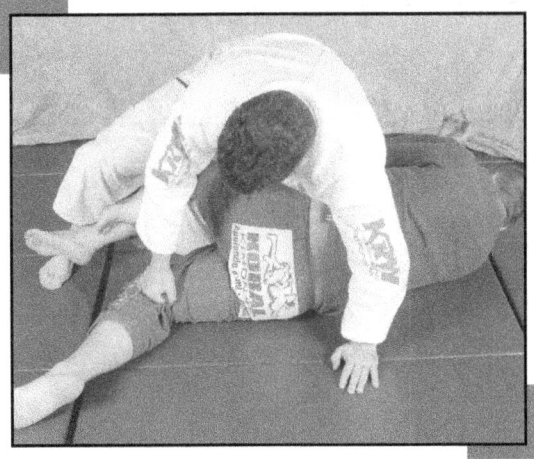

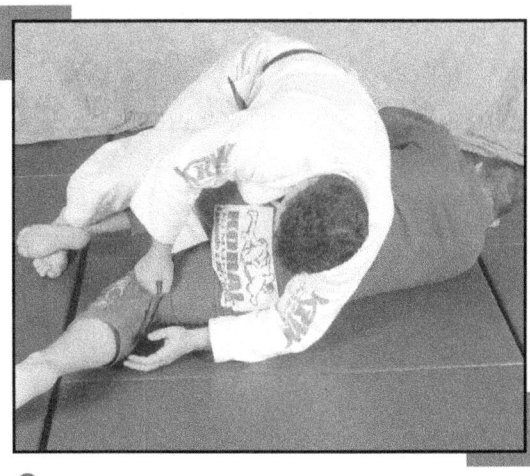

Rigan slides his left leg between the opponent's legs (4), and hooks his left foot under the back of his right knee (5). Then, he leans forward as he maintains a secure grip on the opponent's left leg with his right hand (6).

(continued on next page)

ATTACKS FROM THE GROUND

(continued from previous page)

7

8

9

TECHNIQUE 7

10

Rigan rolls over the opponent's body **(7)** as he simultaneously maintains his body close to the opponent's **(8)**. He keep the lock on the opponent's leg in front of his body, reaches for the opponent's left foot with both of his hands **(9)**, and applies a finishing bent-knee lock **(10)**.

ATTACKS FROM THE GROUND

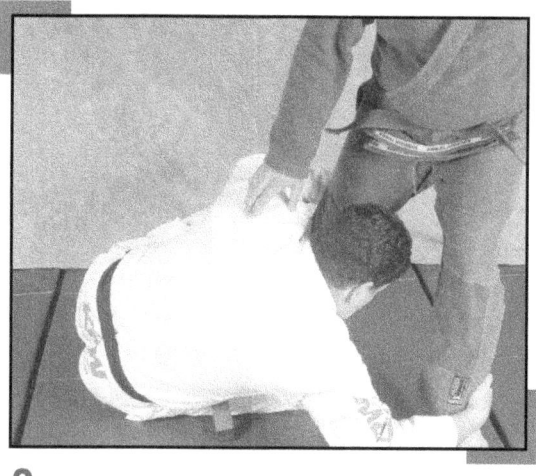

Rigan, seated, faces his opponent, standing (1). Rigan uses his left leg to open the opponent's stance (2) and reaches with his right hand for the opponent's left ankle (3).

TECHNIQUE 8

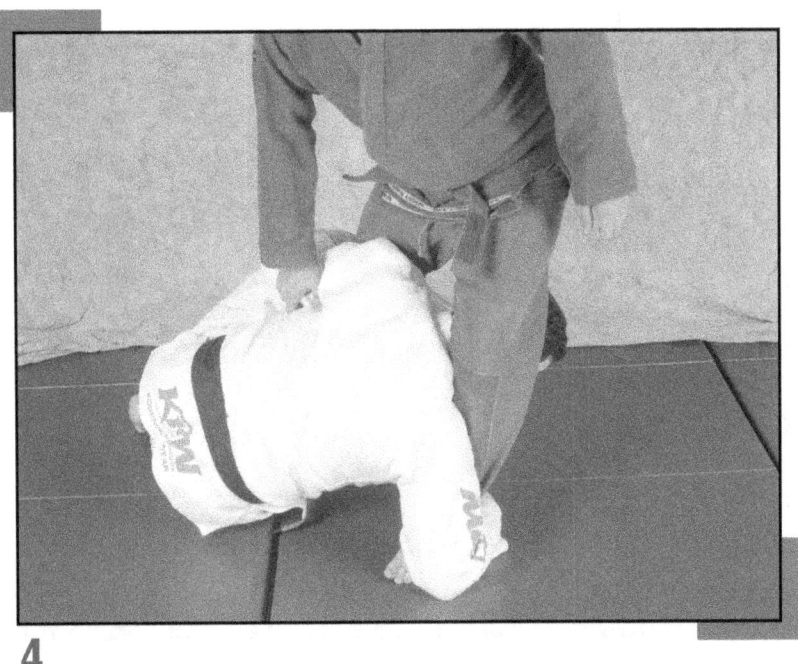

Then, he brings his head between the opponent's legs (4), and pushes forward, applying a takedown (5) that brings the opponent to the ground (6).

(continued on next page)

ATTACKS FROM THE GROUND

(continued from previous page)

7

8

TECHNIQUE 8

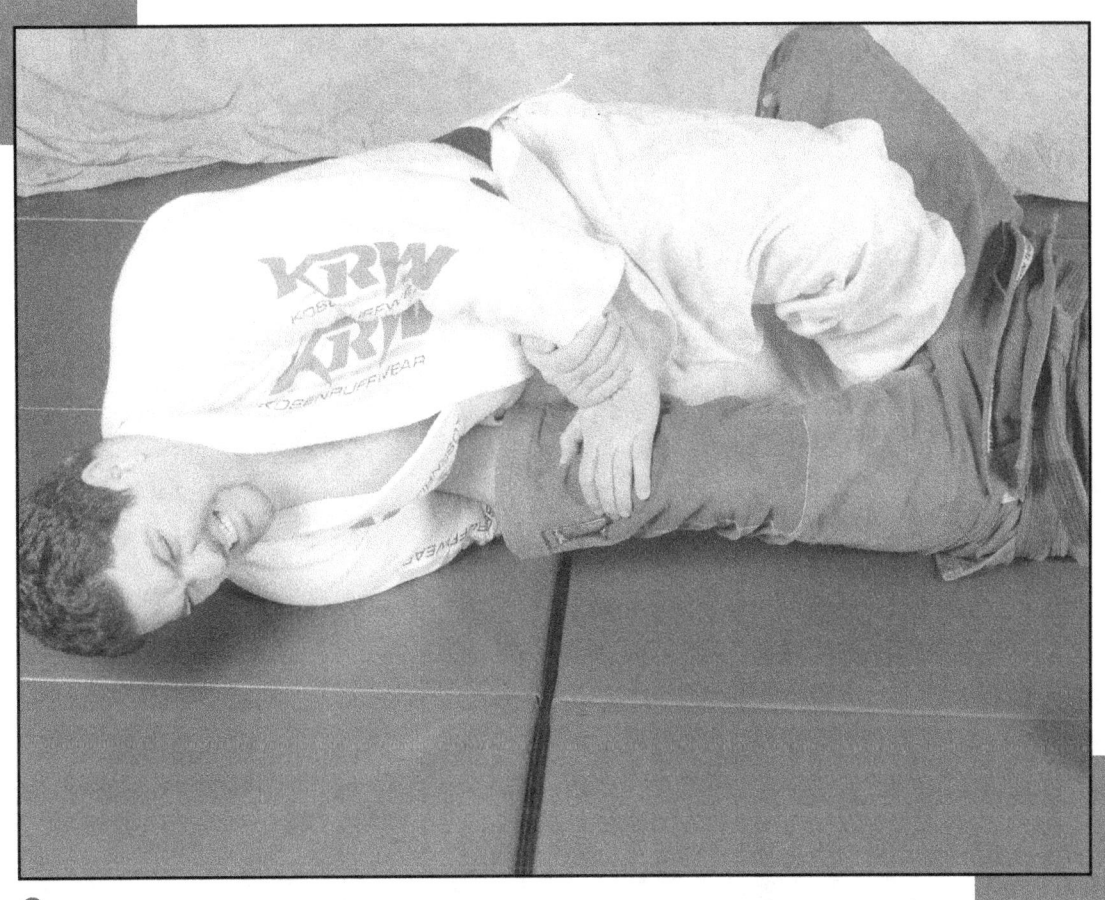

9

Rigan maintains a tight control over the opponent's left ankle as he pushes the opponent's body away with his left hand to prevent him from countering the offensive move (7). Rigan squeezes hard, secures the position of the opponent's hip with his left leg (8), and applies a painful lock to the opponent's left ankle (9).

ATTACKS FROM THE GROUND

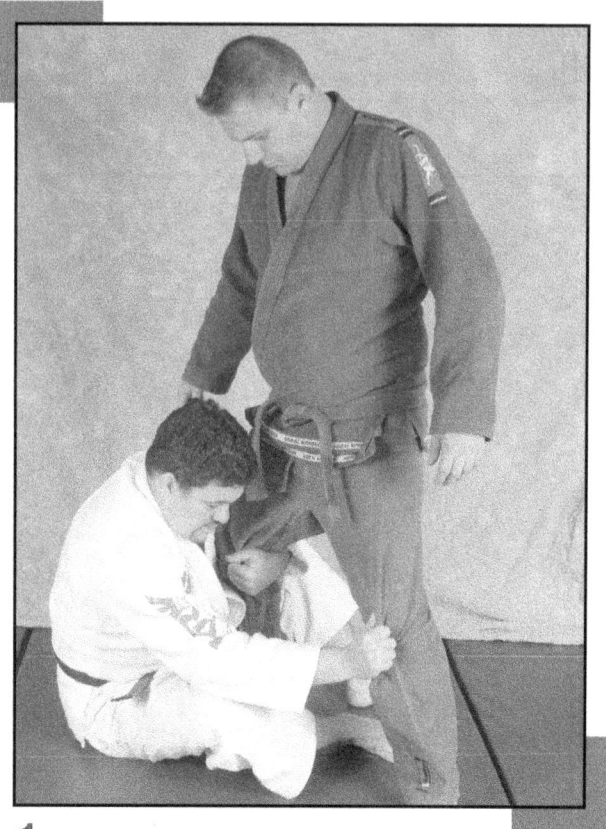

Rigan, seated on the ground, faces his opponent, standing (1). Rigan releases the grip of his right hand, and passes it under the opponent's left leg (2). This gives him leverage to bring his body to the side (3).

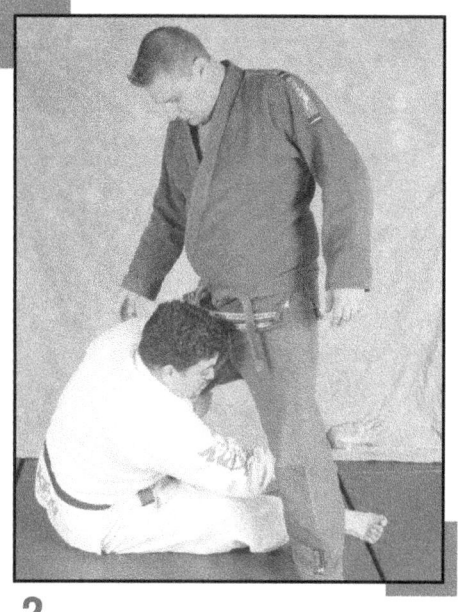

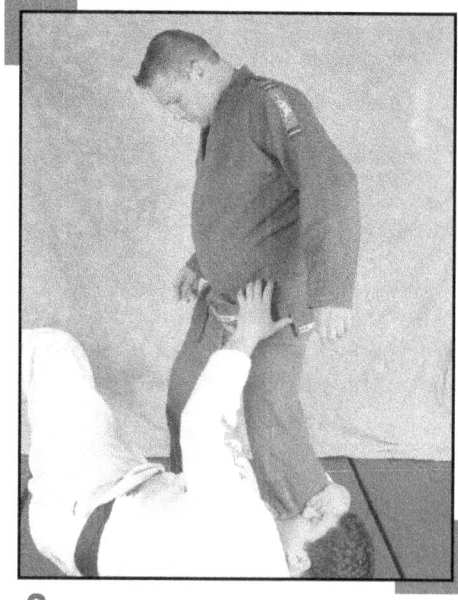

TECHNIQUE 9

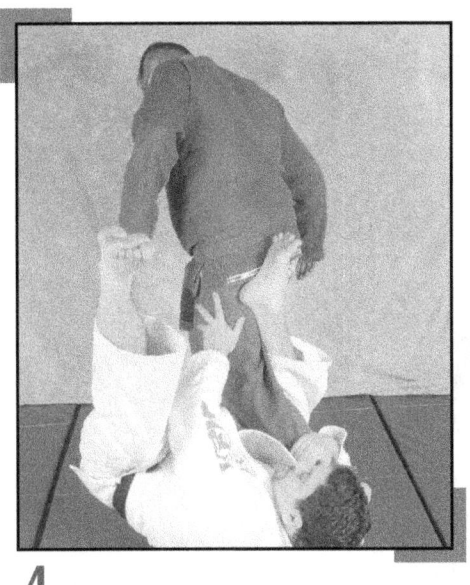
4

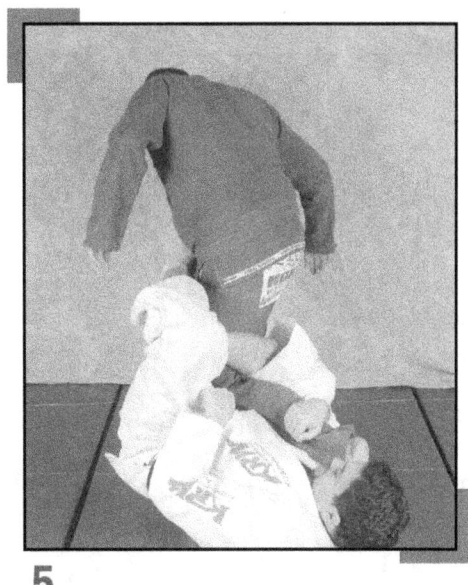
5

6

From that position, Rigan brings his right foot and places it behind the opponent's leg (4). Then, he hooks his right instep under the back of his left knee (5), and pushes forward to bring the opponent to the ground (6).

(continued on next page)

ATTACKS FROM THE GROUND

(continued from previous page)

7

Rigan begins to move his body forward **(7–7A Reverse Angle)**

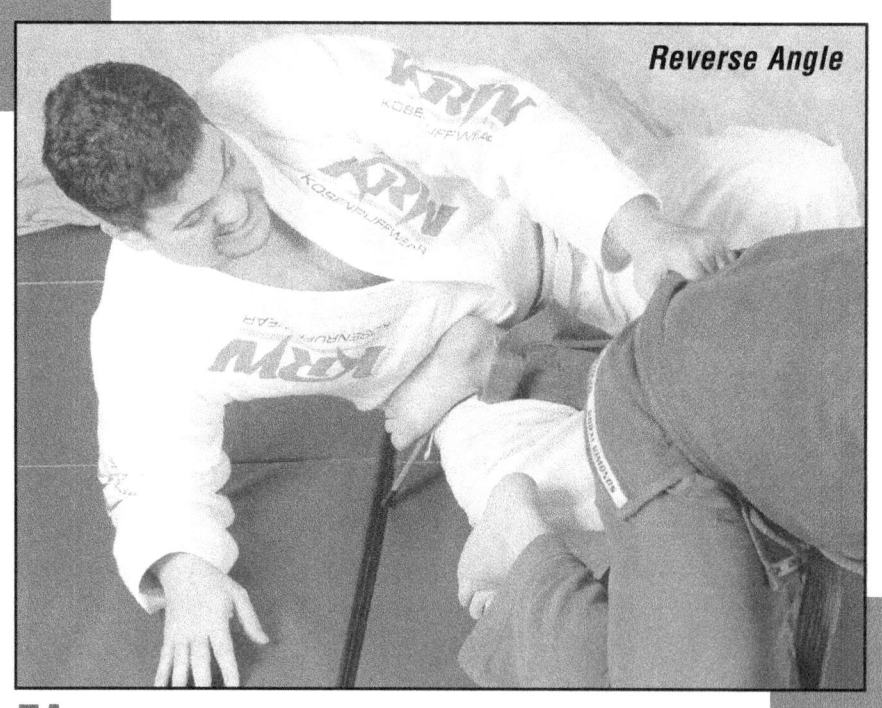

7A

Reverse Angle

TECHNIQUE 9

and grabs the opponent's body to apply the final submission lock (8–8A Reverse Angle).

8

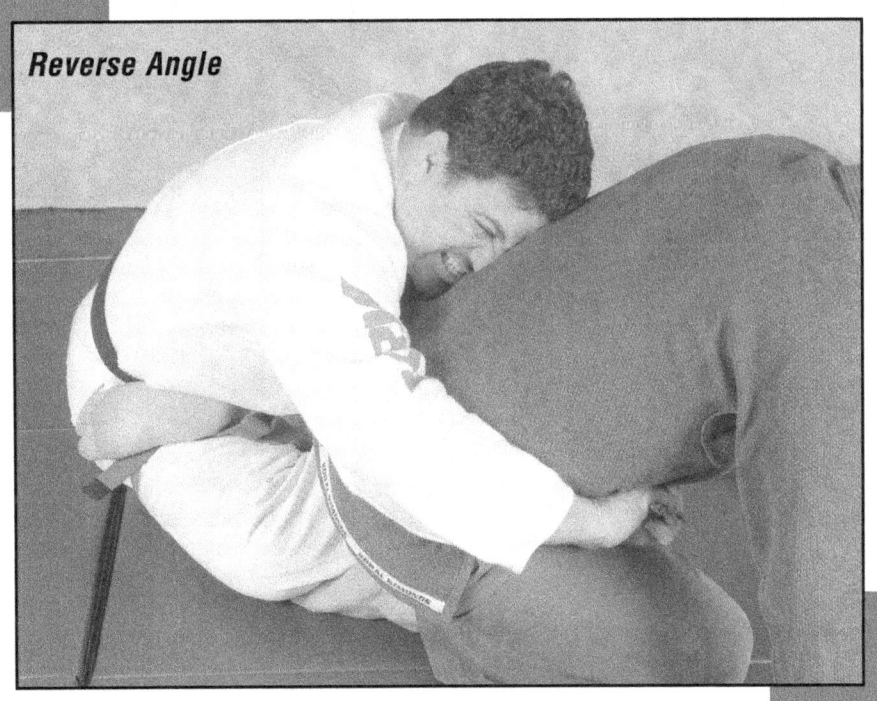

Reverse Angle

8A

ATTACKS FROM THE GROUND

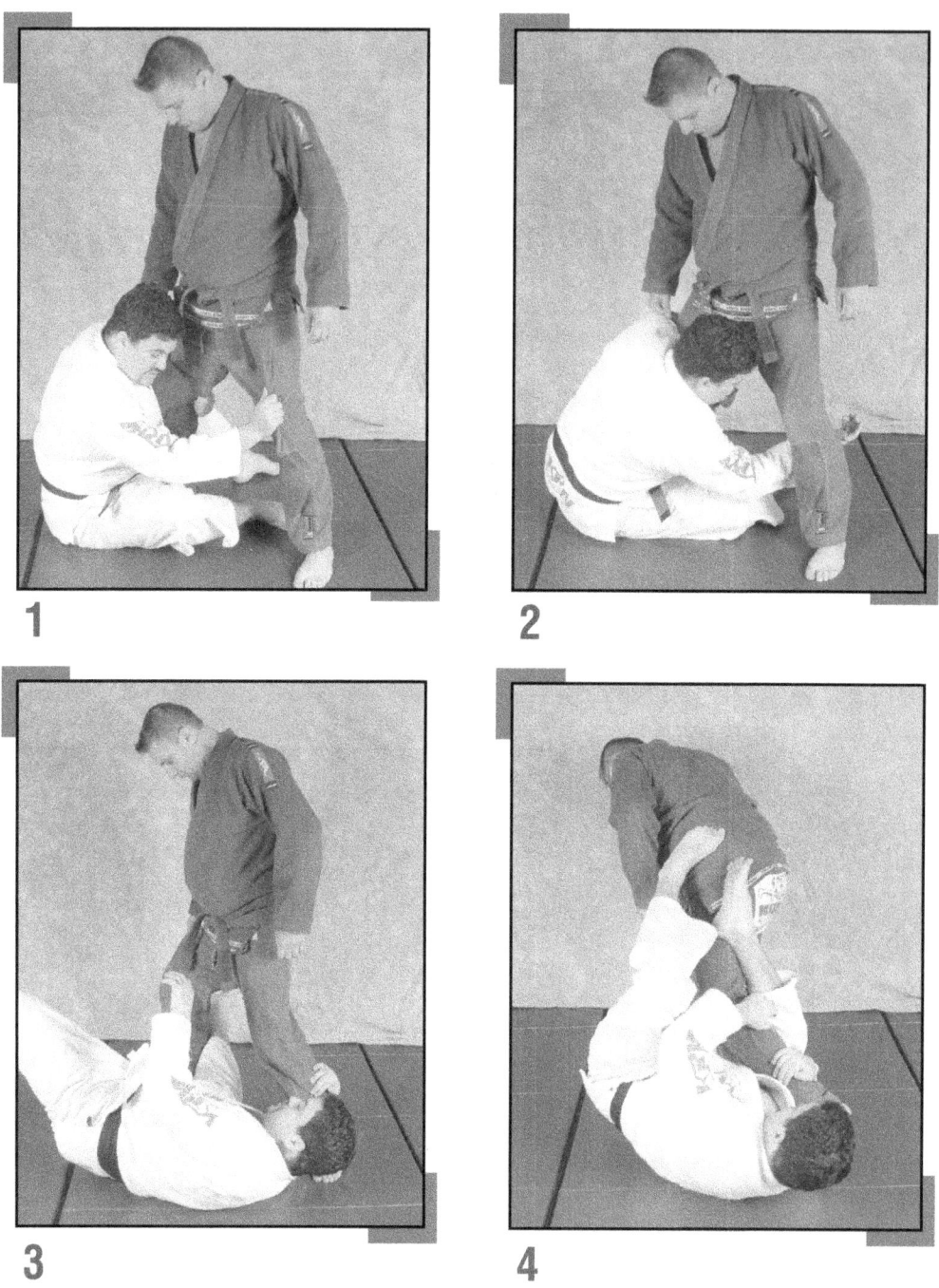

Rigan, seated on the ground, faces his opponent, standing (1). Rigan releases the grip of his right hand and passes it under the opponent's left leg (2). This gives him leverage to bring his body to the side (3) and to pass his right leg around the opponent's left leg as he firmly secures the foot with his right hand (4).

TECHNIQUE 10

Rigan pushes forward and brings the opponent to the ground (5). Then, he applies pressure with his left leg, secures the opponent's left legs between his (6), and applies a footlock (7). Close-up (8).

5

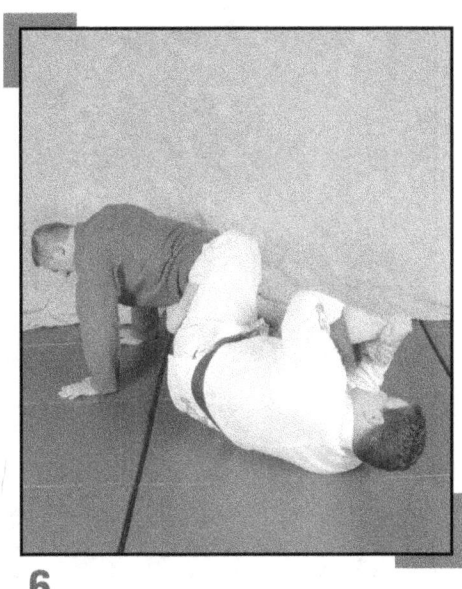
6

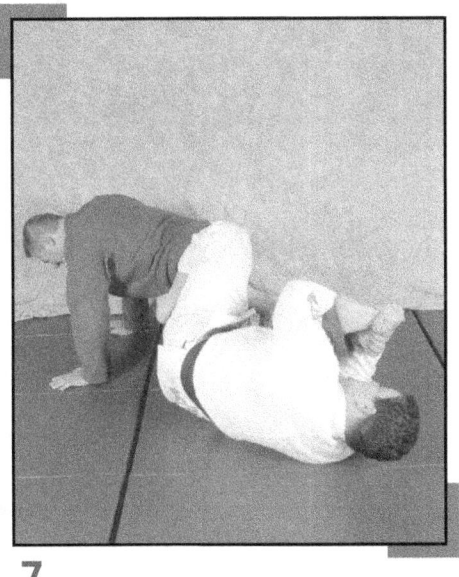
7

8

ATTACKS FROM THE GROUND

Rigan has the opponent in front of him and controls the situation by putting his left foot on the opponent's right hip with the left foot hooked behind the opponent's left knee (1). Rigan releases the grip of his right hand, slides his right leg forward and grabs the opponent's left ankle from behind (2). Then, he brings his right leg to the side and wraps it around the opponent's left leg (3).

1

2

3

TECHNIQUE 11

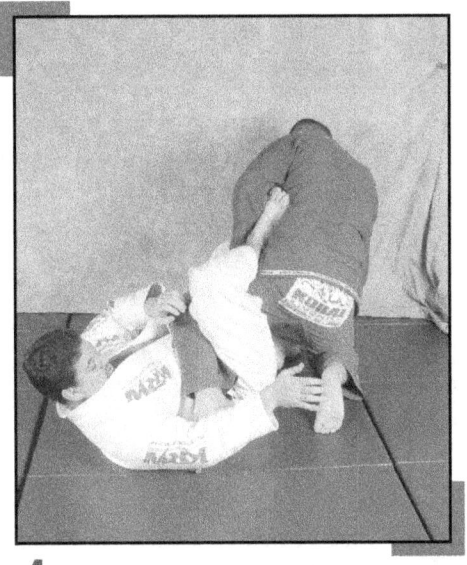

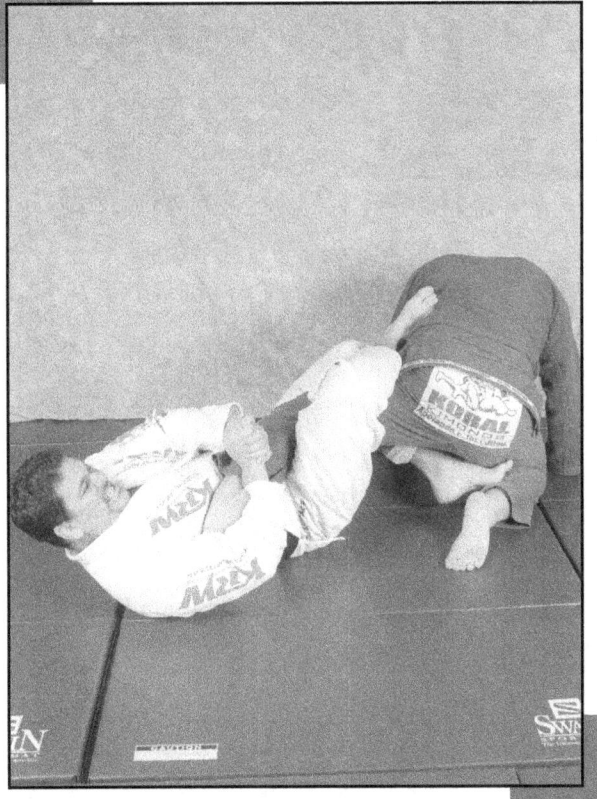

Rigan applies pressure with his right leg and brings his right hand to the outside (4). Then, he grabs the opponent's ankle and holds it right inside his right armpit (5), from where he applies a lock to the opponent's left foot (6).

ATTACKS FROM THE GROUND

Rigan, with a right hand grip on the opponent's left sleeve, has the opponent in front of him and controls the situation by putting his left foot on the opponent's right hip with the left foot hooked behind the opponent's left knee (1). Rigan releases the grip of his right hand, slides his right leg forward, and grabs the opponent's left ankle from behind as he simultaneously pulls down on the opponent's collar with the left hand (2). Then, he brings his right leg to the side and wraps it around the opponent's left leg (3).

Encyclopedia of Leglocks

TECHNIQUE 12

4

5

6

Rigan applies pressure with his right leg and brings his right hand to the inside (4). Then, he reaches out with his left hand and (5) applies a figure-4 lock to the opponent's left foot (6).

ATTACKS FROM THE GROUND

Rigan is trapped inside the opponent's half guard. The opponent has his right foot locked under the back of the left knee (1). Rigan leans over the opponent's chest, and brings his right knee up to break the lock (2). Then, he passes his right hand under the opponent's leg as he simultaneously secures his opponent's left arm with his left hand (3). Now, Rigan brings his left knee over the opponent's stomach (4).

TECHNIQUE 13

5

6

7

Slowly, he brings his body down to the opponent's left side (5) and leans backward as he simultaneously passes his right foot under the back of his left knee (6). Then, he straightens his body and, by pulling the opponent's leg with both hands, applies a knee-bar (7).

ATTACKS FROM THE GROUND

Rigan is trapped inside the opponent's half guard. The opponent has his right foot locked under the back of the left knee (1). Rigan leans over the opponent's chest (2) and brings his right knee up to break the lock (3).

TECHNIQUE 14

He grabs the opponent's left foot with his right hand (4) and passes his left hand under the opponent's leg, reaching his own right wrist (5). From that position, Rigan applies a painful lock to the opponent's left foot (6).

ATTACKS FROM THE GROUND

Rigan is trapped inside the opponent's half guard. The opponent has his right foot locked under the back of the left knee (1). Rigan leans over the opponent's chest and brings his right knee up to break the lock. He grabs the opponent's left foot with his right hand (2). Now, Rigan brings his left knee over the opponent's stomach (3).

TECHNIQUE 15

4

5

6

Slowly, he brings his body down to the opponent's left side (4). The opponent locks his left foot under his right knee to prevent the knee-bar attack (5). Rigan releases the grip and lets the leg go a little bit (6).

(continued on next page)

ATTACKS FROM THE GROUND

(continued from previous page)

7

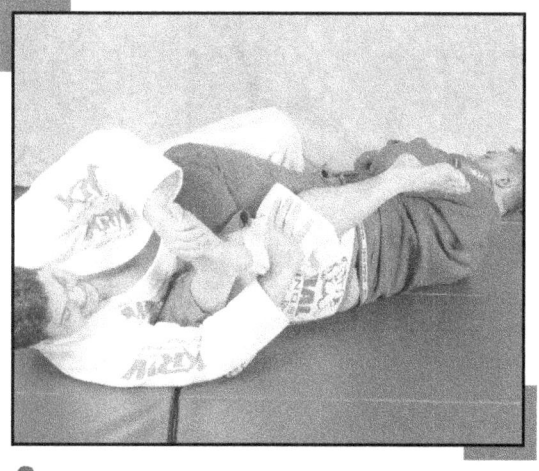
8

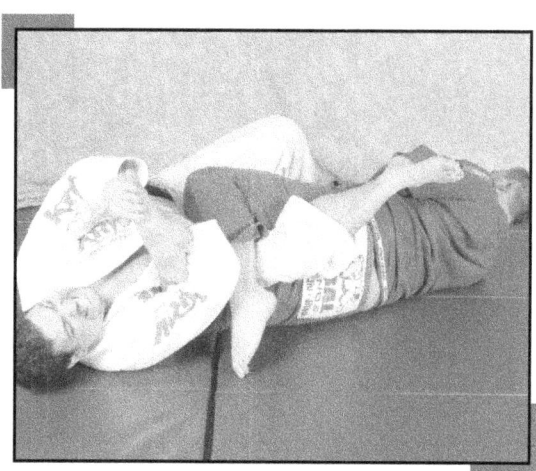
9

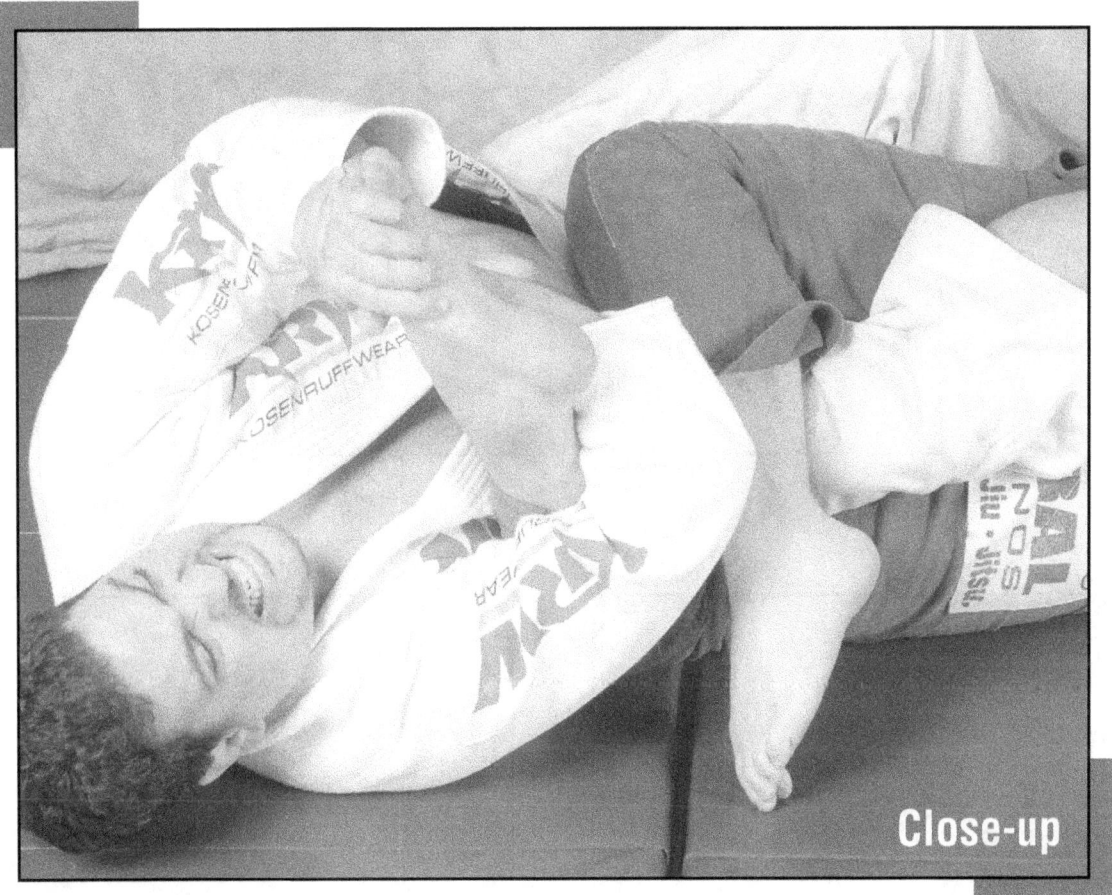

10

Then, he leans forward as he secures the opponent's left foot with his left hand **(7)**. Rigan rolls forward to the other side without losing control of the opponent's foot **(8)**, and applies a figure-4 lock to the foot **(9)**. Close-up **(10)**.

ATTACKS FROM THE GROUND

Rigan is trapped inside the opponent's half guard. The opponent has his right foot locked under the back of the left knee (1). Rigan leans over the opponent's chest and brings his right knee up to break the lock (2). He grabs the opponent's left leg with his right hand (3).

TECHNIQUE 16

4

5

6

Now, Rigan brings his left knee over the opponent's stomach (4). Slowly, he brings his body down to the opponent's left side (5). The opponent locks his left foot under his right knee to prevent the knee-bar attack (6).

(continued on next page)

ATTACKS FROM THE GROUND

(continued from previous page)

7

8

9

This time, Rigan lets the opponent do the action, but hooks his left foot under the opponent's left foot (7). Then he reaches out with his left hand and pulls the opponent's foot close to his body (8). He brings it over the opponent's left foot (9) and applies a lock to the foot with double control on the opponent's legs (10). Close-up (11).

Encyclopedia of Leglocks

TECHNIQUE 16

10

11 Close-up

ATTACKS FROM THE GROUND

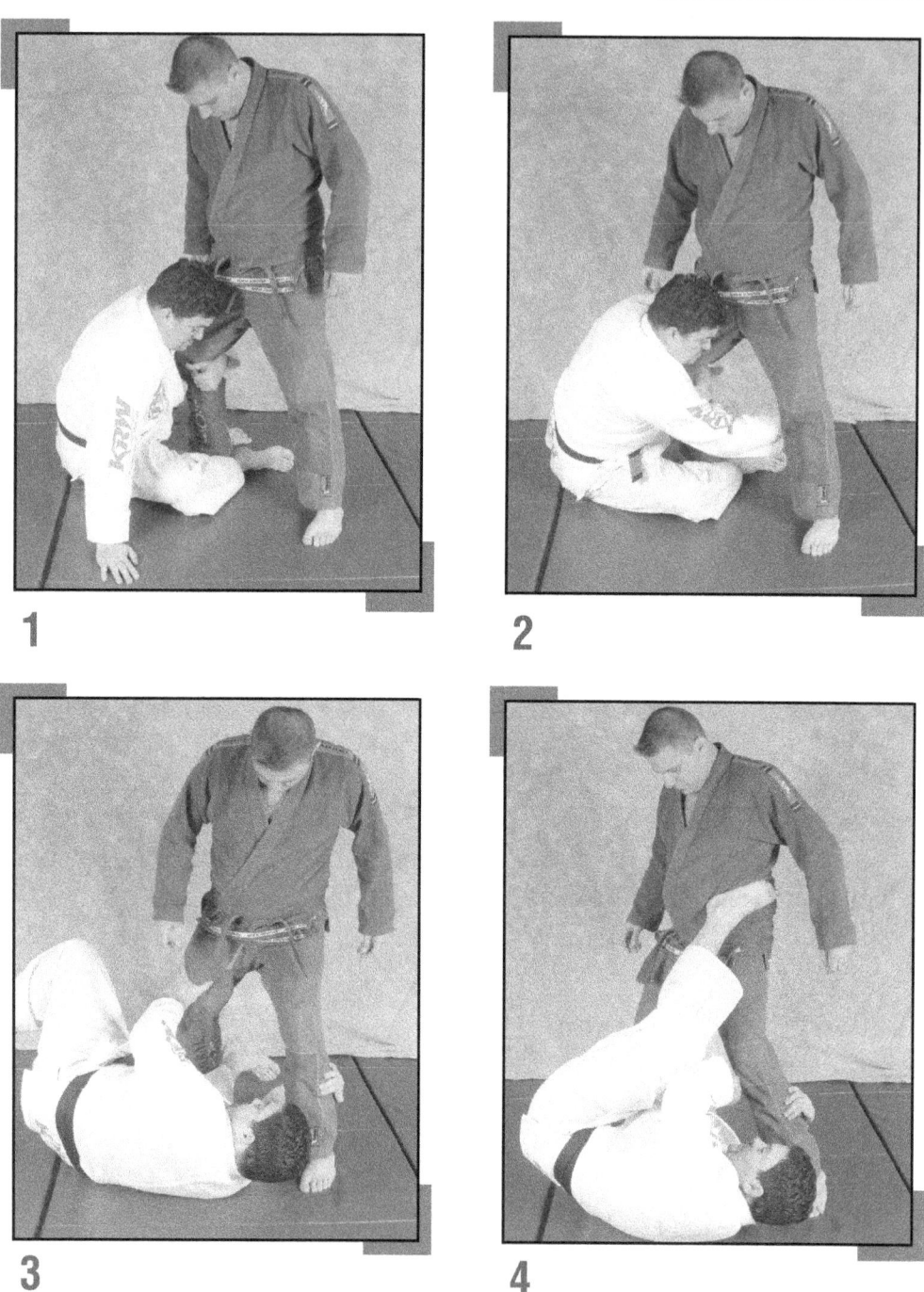

Rigan, seated on the ground, faces his opponent, standing (1). He passes his right hand under the opponent's left leg (2), spins his body to the right (3) and as he simultaneously secures the opponent's left foot, he brings his left leg up to the opponent's left hip (4).

TECHNIQUE 17

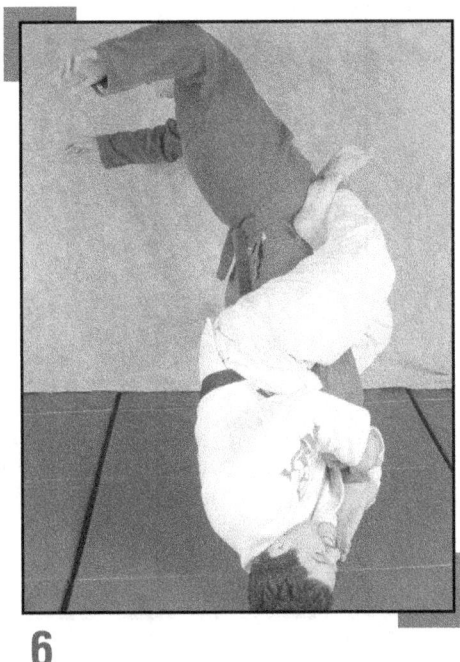

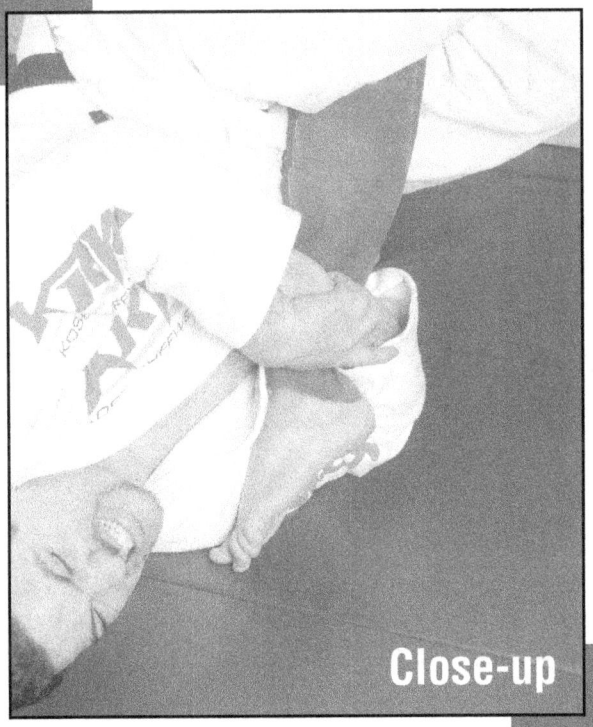

Then, he wraps his right leg around the opponent's left leg (5) and straightens his body to apply a painful knee-bar from the ground (6). Close-up (7).

ATTACKS FROM THE GROUND

Rigan is trapped inside the opponent's half guard. The opponent has his right foot locked under the back of the left knee (1). Rigan leans over the opponent's chest, and brings his right knee up to break the lock (2). Then, he passes his right hand under the opponent's leg (3).

TECHNIQUE 18

4

5

6

Now, Rigan brings his left knee over the opponent's stomach (4). He secures the grip of the opponent's left leg with his right hand and simultaneously controls the right leg, using a hook under the opponent's right knee (5). Then, Rigan reaches with his left hand, grabs the opponent's leg, and pulls it backwards (6).

(continued on next page)

ATTACKS FROM THE GROUND

(continued from previous page)

7

8

TECHNIQUE 18

Close-up

9

Leaning on the right side of his body, Rigan passes his left arm under the opponent's left foot (7) and applies a reverse ankle-lock (8). Close-up (9).

ATTACKS FROM THE GROUND

Rigan is trapped inside the opponent's half guard. The opponent's has his right foot locked under the back of the left knee (1). Rigan leans over the opponent chest, and brings his right knee up to break the lock (2). Then, he passes his right hand under the opponent's leg (3).

TECHNIQUE 19

4

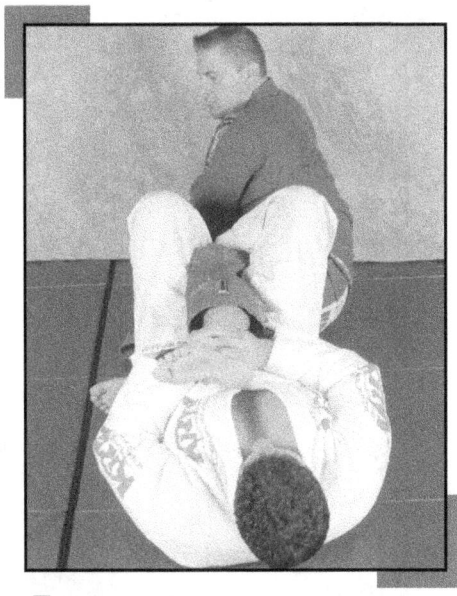
5

6

Rigan brings his left knee over the opponent's stomach (4). He secures the grip of the opponent's left leg with his left hand, but the opponent turns his body to the left, which nullifies the pressure Rigan is putting at the knee level (5). Then, he pulls the opponent's right foot to the right side (6).

(continued on next page)

ATTACKS FROM THE GROUND

(continued from previous page)

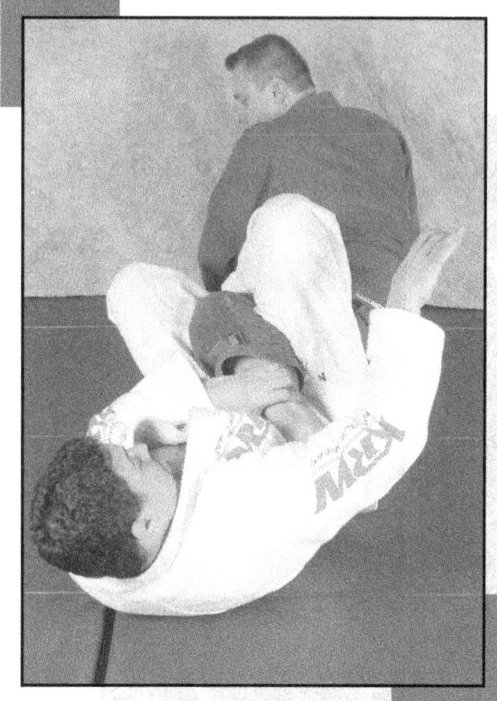
7

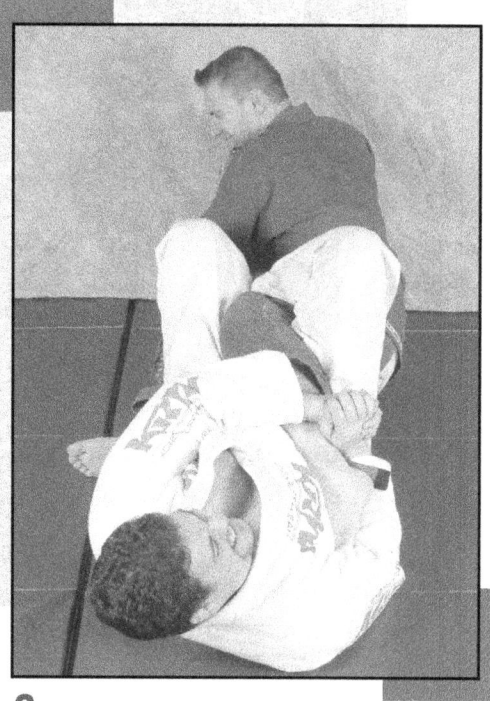
8

TECHNIQUE 19

9

Once under control, Rigan brings his right arm toward the outside (7) and wraps it around the opponent's ankle to apply a lock to the foot (8). Close-up (9).

ATTACKS FROM THE GROUND

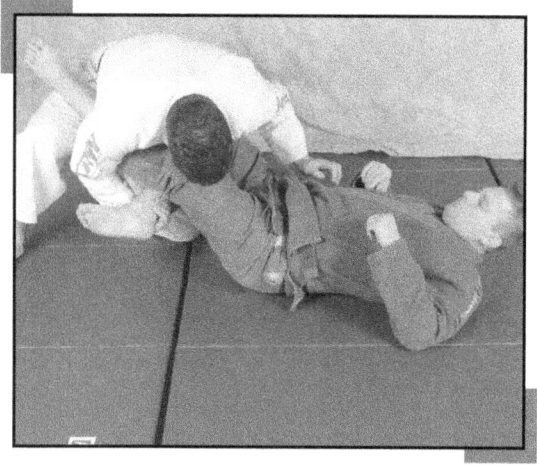

Rigan is facing the opponent's open guard (1). Rigan moves back a little to create space and reaches with his right hand under the opponent's left leg to grab the opponent's right foot (2). He pulls it out as he controls the opponent's left hip with his left hand (3).

4

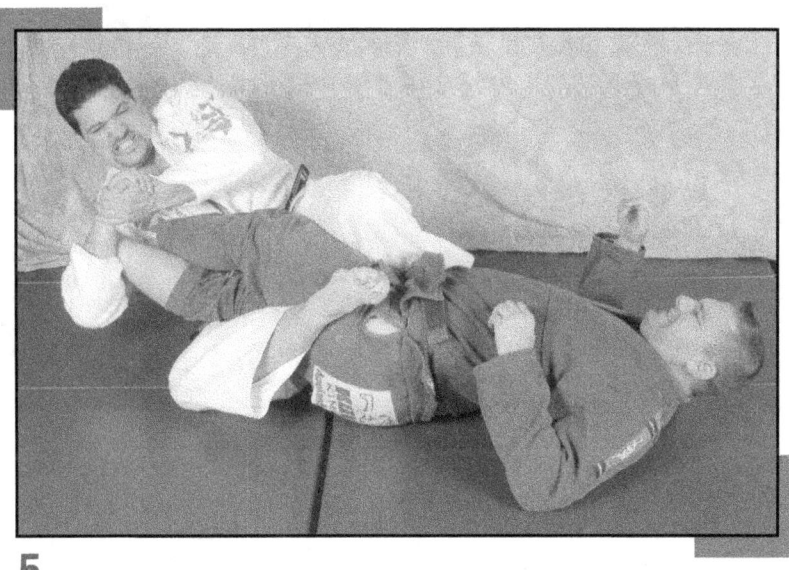

5

Rigan brings his left knee over the opponent's stomach **(4)** and leans back to apply a painful knee-bar with double control of the legs **(5)**.

ATTACKS FROM THE GROUND

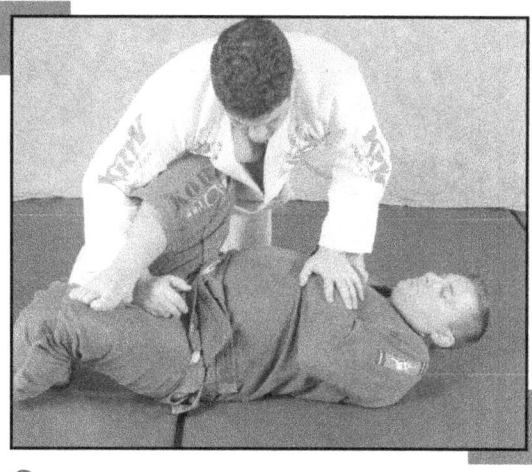

Rigan is fighting his opponent from the side control (1). Rigan moves his left hand and brings it up to control the opponent's left arm (2). Then, he passes his right hand under the opponent's right leg as he applies pressure with his chest to have better control of the opponent's leg (3).

TECHNIQUE 21

4

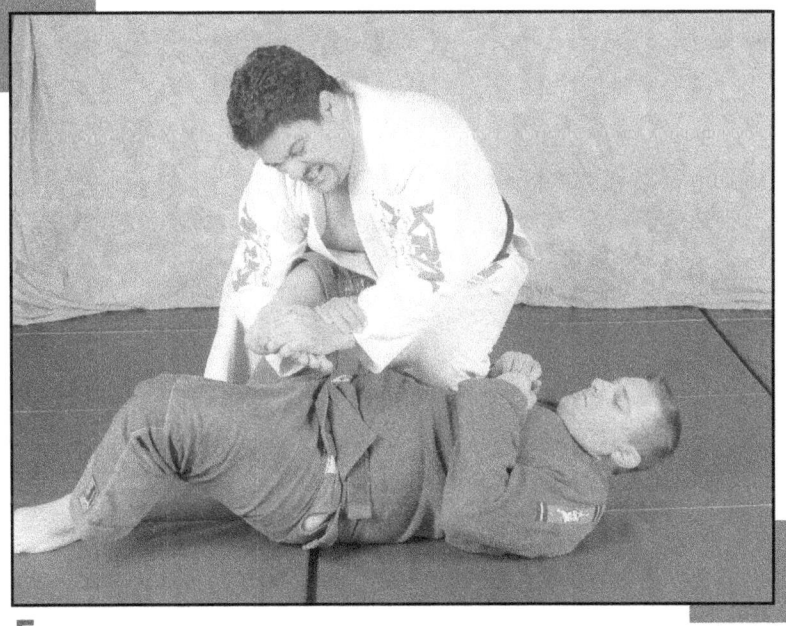

5

Rigan brings his left hand under his right (4) and, by grabbing his own left wrist, applies a painful figure-4 lock to the foot (5).

ATTACKS FROM THE GROUND

Rigan has the opponent in his side control position (1). He creates space to (2) bring the right knee up as he passes his right hand under the opponent's right leg (3).

TECHNIQUE 22

Rigan brings his left knee on top of the opponent's stomach as secures his left arm with the left hand (4). Maintaining close control of the leg, Rigan leans backwards, straightens the opponent's leg (5), and applies a painful knee-bar (6).

ATTACKS FROM THE GROUND

Rigan has the opponent in his side control position (1). The opponent moves his right knee inside to put Rigan inside the guard (2). As soon as Rigan feels the move, he brings his hips closer (3), and puts his trunk up as he secures his position, using both hands (4).

1

2

3

4

TECHNIQUE 23

5

6

7

8

Now, Rigan brings his right knee up and locks the opponent's right leg between his right thigh and his stomach (5). Then, he leans back as he maintains control of the opponent's leg (6) and begins to straighten the leg (7), until he finally applies perfect knee-bar submission by helping to put pressure, using his left foot on the opponent's left thigh (8).

ATTACKS FROM THE GROUND

1

2

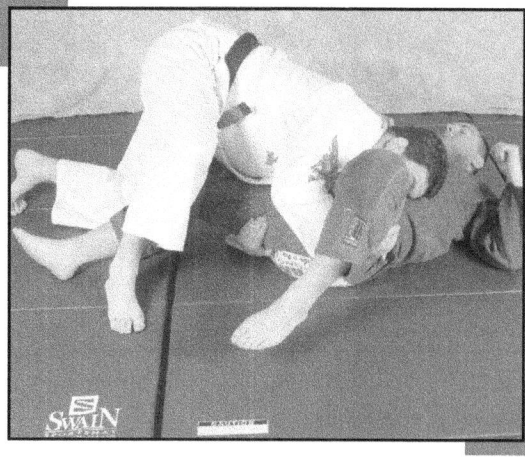
3

Rigan is on top of the opponent but the opponent has both feet inside Rigan's thighs (1). Rigan uses his left hand to grab the opponent's right leg as he simultaneously brings his hips back to create space (2), so he can move his right leg to the left and pass the right arm under the opponent's left leg (3).

TECHNIQUE 24

4

5

6

Rigan uses his right foot to hook the opponent's right foot (4) and traps it between his own legs (5), so he can apply a straight knee-bar to his opponent's right leg (6).

ATTACKS FROM THE GROUND

Rigan has both of his opponent's feet inside of his legs (1). He moves his body to the left side and slides his hips to create space, so he can bring the right knee back and wrap the opponent's right leg with his left hand (2). Then, he uses his right knee to push the opponent's right foot back to the front (3) and, lifting his right knee, he traps the foot between his stomach and his right thigh (4).

1

2

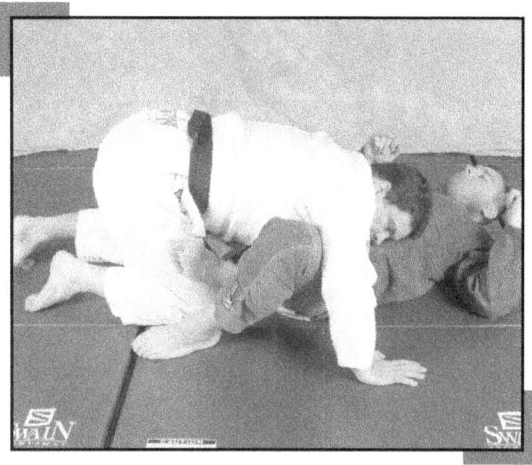

3

4

TECHNIQUE 25

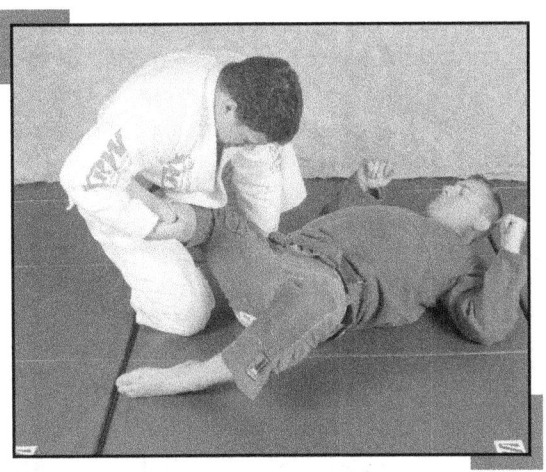
5

6

7

8

Rigan brings his right knee to the ground and lifts the left knee up to balance his position (5). Then, without letting the opponent's right foot go, Rigan leans back (6), keeps tight control over the opponent's leg by squeezing hard with his right thigh and putting downward pressure with his left foot (7), and applies a lock to the opponent's right ankle (8).

ATTACKS FROM THE GROUND

Rigan is trying to pass the opponent's guard (1), but the opponent is pushing him away with his right hand (2). Rigan wraps the opponent's right leg around with his left arm and stands up as he reaches out to grab his own left hand with his right hand (3). Then, he takes a little step and moves his right foot close to the opponent's left hip (4).

1

2

3

4

5

6

7

Now, he sits back on the ground but maintains tight control of the opponent's right leg by keeping the leg trapped between his arms and body (5). Then, he brings his right leg over the opponent's right thigh and then puts his left leg over his right to create pressure (6). By leaning back and putting forward pressure with his legs, Rigan applies a painful leglock to his opponent (7).

ATTACKS FROM THE GROUND

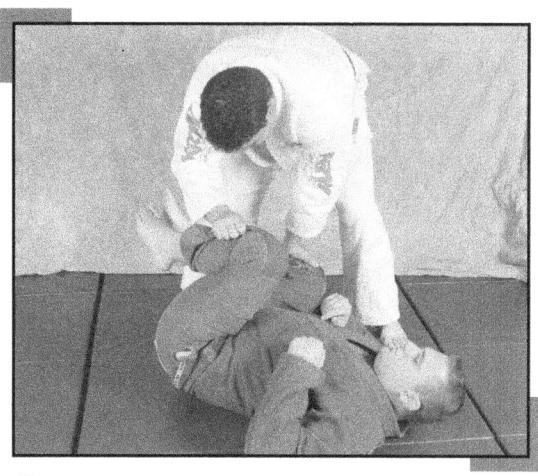

Rigan is facing his opponent's open guard (1). Rigan moves to his left and tries to avoid the guard (2) by controlling both legs as he simultaneously circles to the opponent's right side (3).

TECHNIQUE 27

4

5

6

Once on the side, he grabs the opponent's left foot (4) and starts reaching out (5) to put his left hand on the ground (6).

(continued on next page)

ATTACKS FROM THE GROUND

(continued from previous page)

7

8

9

10

Then, he rolls to the other side (7) and, without losing control of the opponent's left foot (8), he lands on his back, establishes his position (9), and applies a painful figure-4 lock to the opponent's foot (10).

ATTACKS FROM THE GROUND

Rigan is on the north-south position with his opponent (1). The opponent pushes him away with both arms (2) so he can bring his legs up to try to escape (3).

10

Then, he rolls to the other side **(7)** and, without losing control of the opponent's left foot **(8)**, he lands on his back, establishes his position **(9)**, and applies a painful figure-4 lock to the opponent's foot **(10)**.

ATTACKS FROM THE GROUND

Rigan is on the north-south position with his opponent (1). The opponent pushes him away with both arms (2) so he can bring his legs up to try to escape (3).

TECHNIQUE 28

4

5

6

Rigan feels the push and let the legs go but maintains his hips close to the opponent without giving up distance (4). Then, he grabs the opponent's left foot with his right hand and wraps the left calf with his left hand (5), to apply a figure-4 footlock (6).

ATTACKS FROM THE GROUND

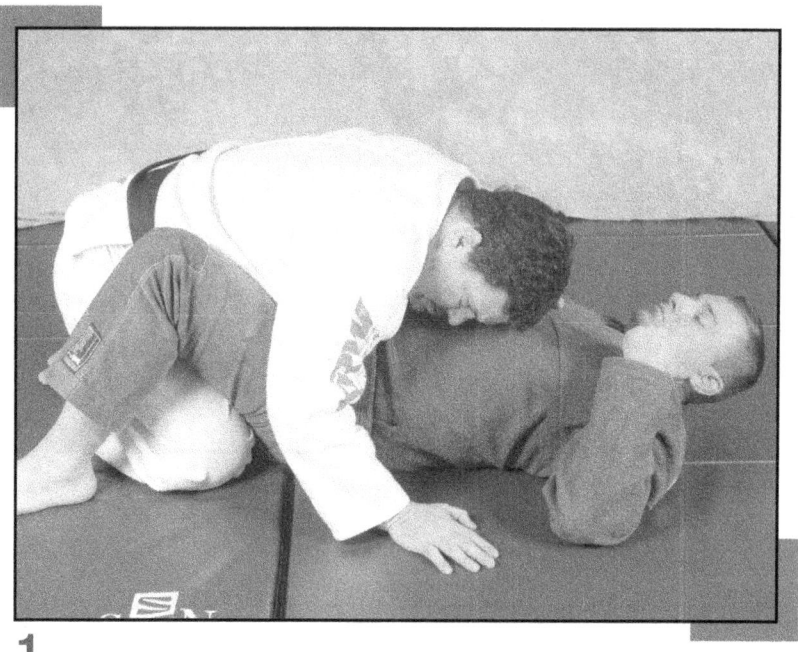

Rigan is inside the opponent's open guard (1). He brings his right knee up and lifts the opponent's left foot (2). Then, with his right hand, Rigan grabs the instep of the foot as he pushes the opponent down by using his left hand on the opponent's chest (3).

TECHNIQUE 29

He brings his left hand around the opponent's left calf (4) and grabs his right wrist with his left hand (5). Then, he turns his body to the side and applies pressure to finish the opponent off with a footlock (6).

ATTACKS FROM THE GROUND

Rigan, standing, faces the opponent's open guard (1). Rigan pushes the opponent's right leg down to create space for his left knee to pass the guard (2). Then, he begins to turn his body to the right as he simultaneously uses his left hand to keep his balance during the movement (3). As he passes his body to the other side, Rigan maintains tight control of the opponent's left leg (4).

1

2

3

4

TECHNIQUE 30

5

6

7

Then, he brings his left foot to the outside of the opponent's left hip (5), sits down as he grabs the opponent's leg with both hands (6), and applies a painful knee-bar (7).

ATTACKS FROM THE GROUND

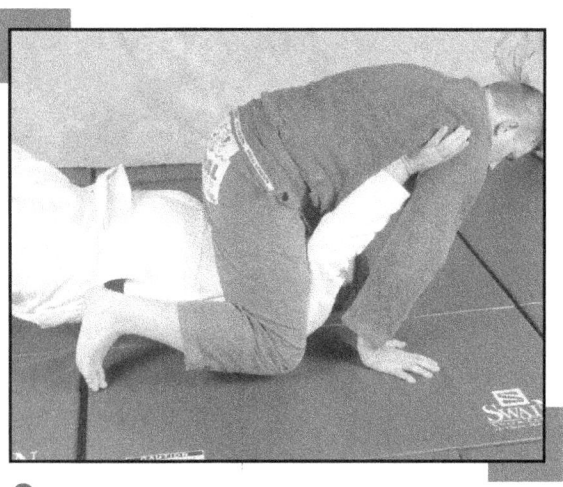
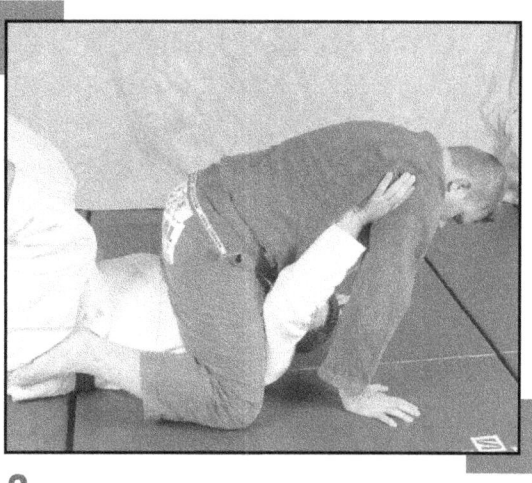

Rigan is under the opponent's mount position (1). Rigan uses his arms to push the opponent away as he simultaneously arches his back to bring him forward (2). Once the space has been created, he begins to bring his legs up (3).

TECHNIQUE 31

4

5

With both feet placed under the opponent's armpits (4), Rigan pushes hard and slides his trunk under the opponent's body (5). Then, he leans to the left side and begins to pull his body from under the opponent (6).

6

(continued on next page)

ATTACKS FROM THE GROUND

(continued from previous page)

While maintaining tight control of the opponent's trunk by using his legs (7), Rigan begins to stand up as he wraps his left arm around the opponent's left foot (8). Then, he sits down on the opponent's body (9).

TECHNIQUE 31

10

11

With tight control of the opponent's body, Rigan brings his left hand to grab his own right wrist to apply a figure-4 footlock (10). If the opponent turns around and releases his foot from the lock, Rigan can change the grip and apply a lock to the ankle by modifying the angle of the grip and turning his body to the left (11). Close-up (12).

Close-up
12

ATTACKS FROM THE GROUND

The opponent has Rigan under control on the mounted position (1). Rigan begins to move his body to create space (2) and slides his right hip to the side as he pushes the opponent's right hip away (3).

TECHNIQUE 32

4

5

Rigan now slides his right hip away to the side (4) and brings his right leg to the outside (5). Then, he puts his right leg over the opponent's left leg (6).

6

(continued on next page)

ATTACKS FROM THE GROUND

(continued from previous page)

7

8

TECHNIQUE 32

9

Rigan pushes the opponent's body away with his right leg **(7)** as he keeps tight control of the left foot to apply an anklelock **(8)**. Close-up **(9)**.

ATTACKS FROM THE GROUND

Rigan has the opponent in the closed guard but the opponent is standing ready to pass the guard (1). Rigan brings his left hand to grab the opponent's left sleeve to make sure he won't be able to stop his next move (2). Then, he passes his right hand around the opponent's left ankle (3).

TECHNIQUE 33

Rigan reaches with his left hand and, with the right hand, grabs the opponent's left sleeve (4) so he can control both the left hand and the left leg (5) with only one grip of his right hand (6).

(continued on next page)

ATTACKS FROM THE GROUND

(continued from previous page)

7

8

9

He brings the opponent to the ground and begins what seems to be an omoplata attack **(7)**. He locks the opponent' left arm with his legs **(8)** and reaches for the left leg with his left hand **(9)**.

TECHNIQUE 33

10

11

Then, Rigan passes his left hand behind the opponent's Achilles tendon (10), and applies a footlock (11).

ATTACKS FROM THE GROUND

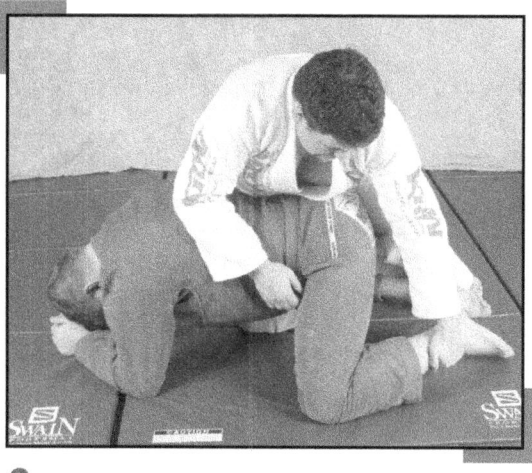

Rigan is trying to attack the opponent's back (1). The opponent covers well and Rigan decides to turn his body to the left (2). Then, he grabs the opponent's left foot with his left hand as he simultaneously hooks the opponent's leg with his right leg (3).

TECHNIQUE 34

4

5

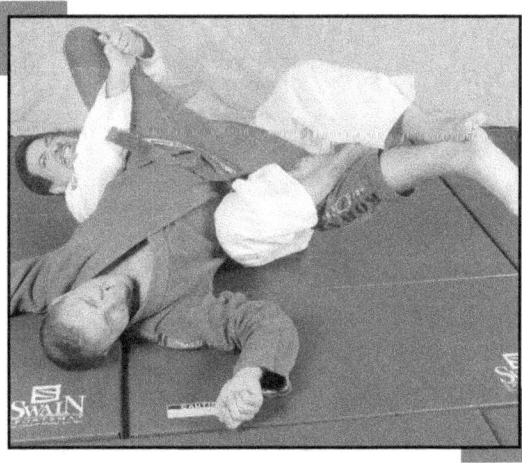

6

Rigan leans backward on his back and pulls the opponent all the way back, without releasing any of the grips (4). Then, he passes his left hand under the opponent's left thigh (5) and applies a hip lock to the opponent (6).

ATTACKS FROM THE GROUND

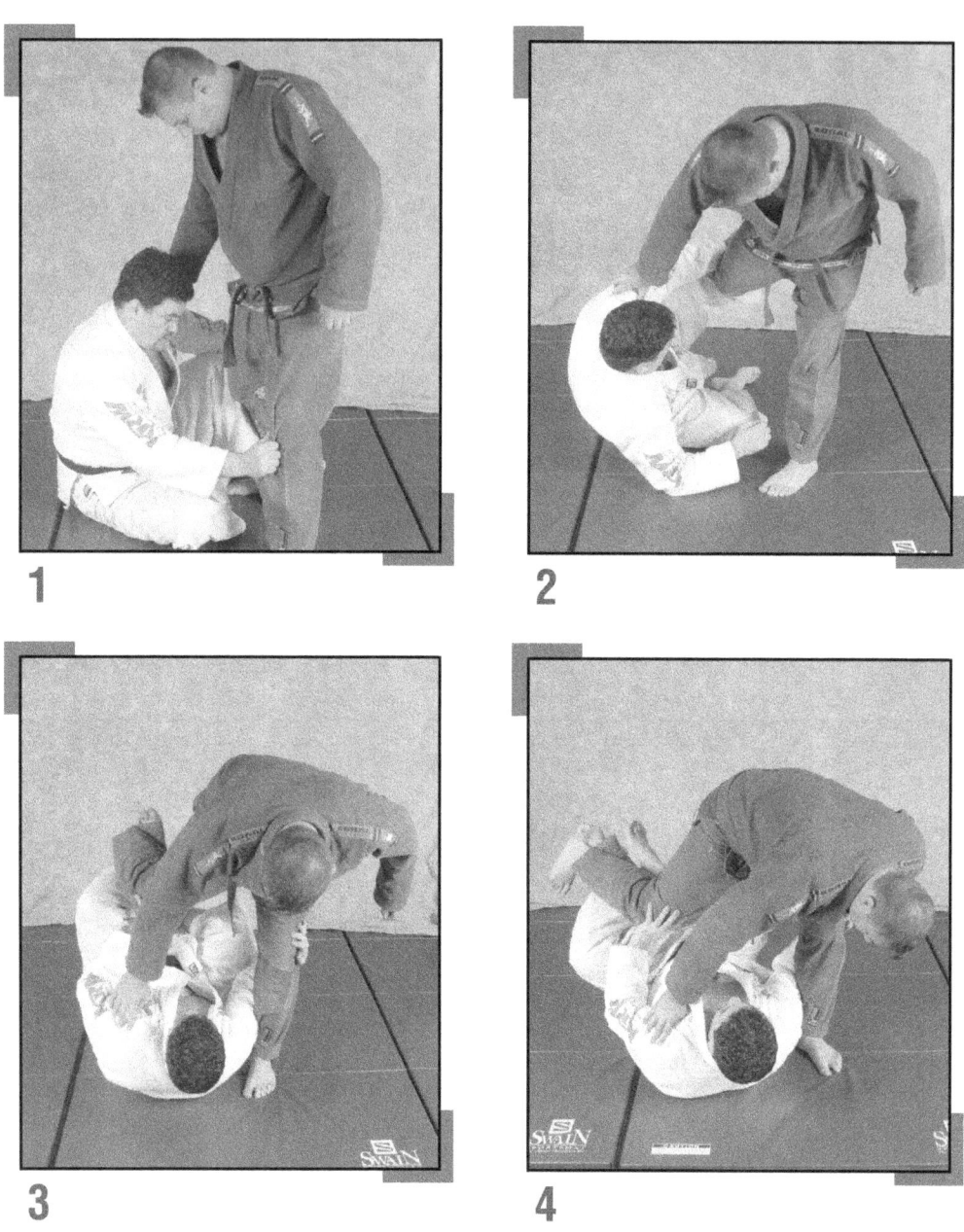

Rigan, seated on the ground, faces his opponent, standing (1). Rigan lifts the opponent's right leg, using a hooking action of his left foot (2), which creates space for him to slide his body under the opponent's legs (3-4).

TECHNIQUE 35

Once under the opponent's body, Rigan passes his right hand around the opponent's left leg **(5)** and, by simultaneously pulling from the opponent's right sleeve with his left hand **(6)**, he brings him to the ground, using his right foot in a hooking action **(7)**.

5

6

7

(continued on next page)

ATTACKS FROM THE GROUND

(continued from previous page)

8

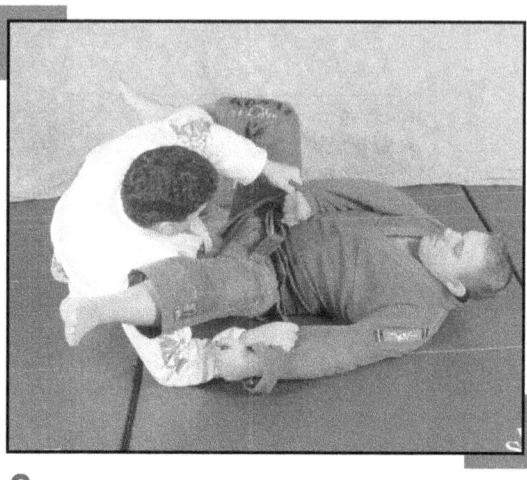

9

10

11

With the opponent fallen on the ground (8), Rigan turns around (9) and starts facing the opponent as he manages to maintain the opponent's left leg over his right shoulder (10). Then, he reaches with his right hand and grabs the opponent's collar (11).

TECHNIQUE 35

12

Rigan moves forward and puts pressure by leaning all his body weight on top of the opponent's chest. He keeps the opponent's right leg straight and inside his right arm, which creates additional pressure to the painful position **(12)**.

ATTACKS FROM THE GROUND

Rigan controls the opponent from the side position **(1)**. Using his right arm, he brings the opponent's right leg closer to his body **(2)**. Then, he passes his right leg over the opponent's left leg **(3)**. Now, he grabs the opponent's right leg from behind **(4)**.

1

2

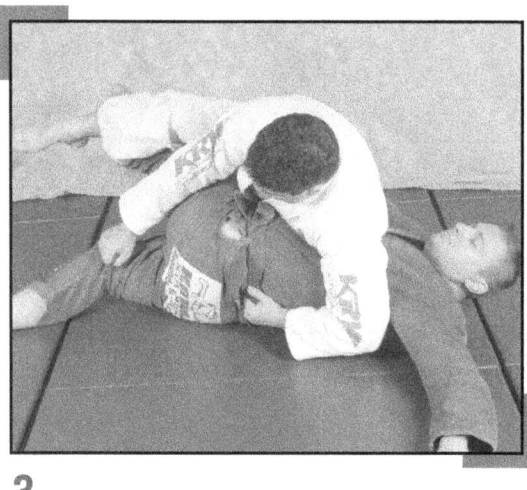

3

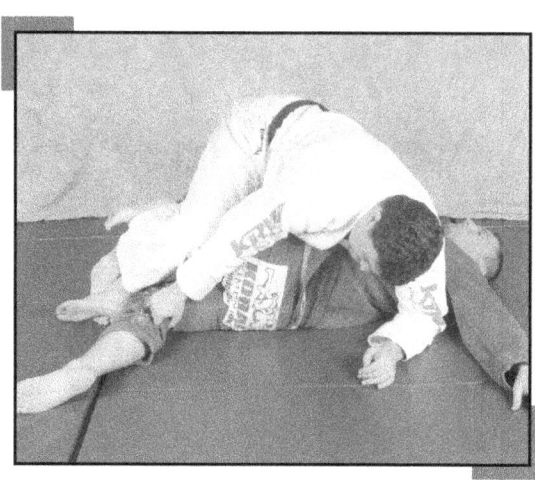

4

TECHNIQUE 36

5

6

7

8

Rigan rolls forward over the opponent's body as he simultaneously hooks the opponent's left leg with his right foot (5). As soon as the opponent's leg passes his over his body (6), Rigan grabs the opponent's other leg with his right hand and secures the left leg by closing a trap with his own legs (7). Then, he applies a painful hip lock to the opponent (8).

ATTACKS FROM THE GROUND

1

2 3

Rigan controls the opponent from the side (1). He uses his right hand to grab the opponent's left leg (2) and begins to pass his left leg over the opponent (3).

TECHNIQUE 37

Once the left foot touches the ground (4), Rigan establishes his positions and sits on the opponent's stomach (5). Then, he grabs both of the opponent's legs with his arms and pulls upwards (6).

(continued on next page)

ATTACKS FROM THE GROUND

(continued from previous page)

7

8

ATTACKS FROM THE GROUND

(continued from previous page)

7

8

TECHNIQUE 37

Once the left foot touches the ground (4), Rigan establishes his positions and sits on the opponent's stomach (5). Then, he grabs both of the opponent's legs with his arms and pulls upwards (6).

(continued on next page)

TECHNIQUE 37

9

As soon as he feels that the opponent is trying to push down with the leg to escape from the position, Rigan lets go one leg but keeps the other under control with his left hand **(7)**. Then, he slides to the side **(8)**, and ends up lying on the ground and applying a devastating knee-bar to the opponent's left leg **(9)**.

ATTACKS FROM THE GROUND

Rigan has the opponent under control from the side (1). He uses his left hand to support his body and brings the right knee on top of the opponent's stomach (2). Once he is secure in that position and fully controls the opponent's body movement (3), he pivots on his right knee (4).

1

2

3

4

TECHNIQUE 38

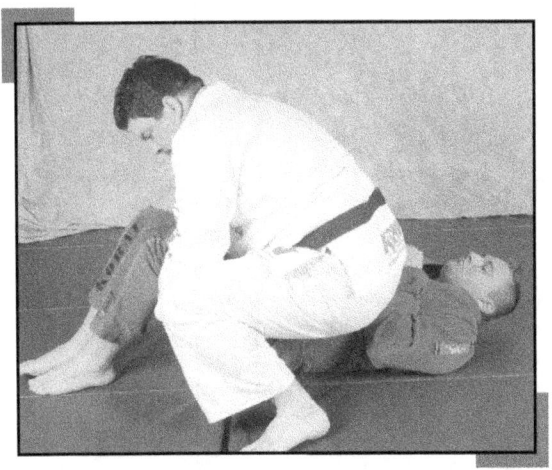
5

6

7 8

By bringing his left leg to the other side of the opponent's body **(5)**, Rigan sits down on the opponent's stomach and grabs one of his legs **(6)**. Then, he slides his body to the left side, hooks his right foot under the back of the knee of his left leg **(7)**, and applies a knee-bar to his opponent **(8)**.

ATTACKS FROM THE GROUND

Rigan has the opponent inside of the close guard (1). Rigan brings his right arm to the side and hooks the opponent's left leg with his right hand (2). Then, he opens the guard and, as he pushes the opponent's right shoulder away with the left hand, he begins to pivot to the right (3).

TECHNIQUE 39

4

5

6

Now, Rigan brings his left leg over the opponent's head and to the left side of the neck **(4)**, but instead of attacking with an armlock from that position, he passes the leg all the way to the right side **(5)** and, by pulling the opponent's left foot toward his body and straightening his hips, applies a painful knee-bar **(6)**.

ATTACKS FROM THE GROUND

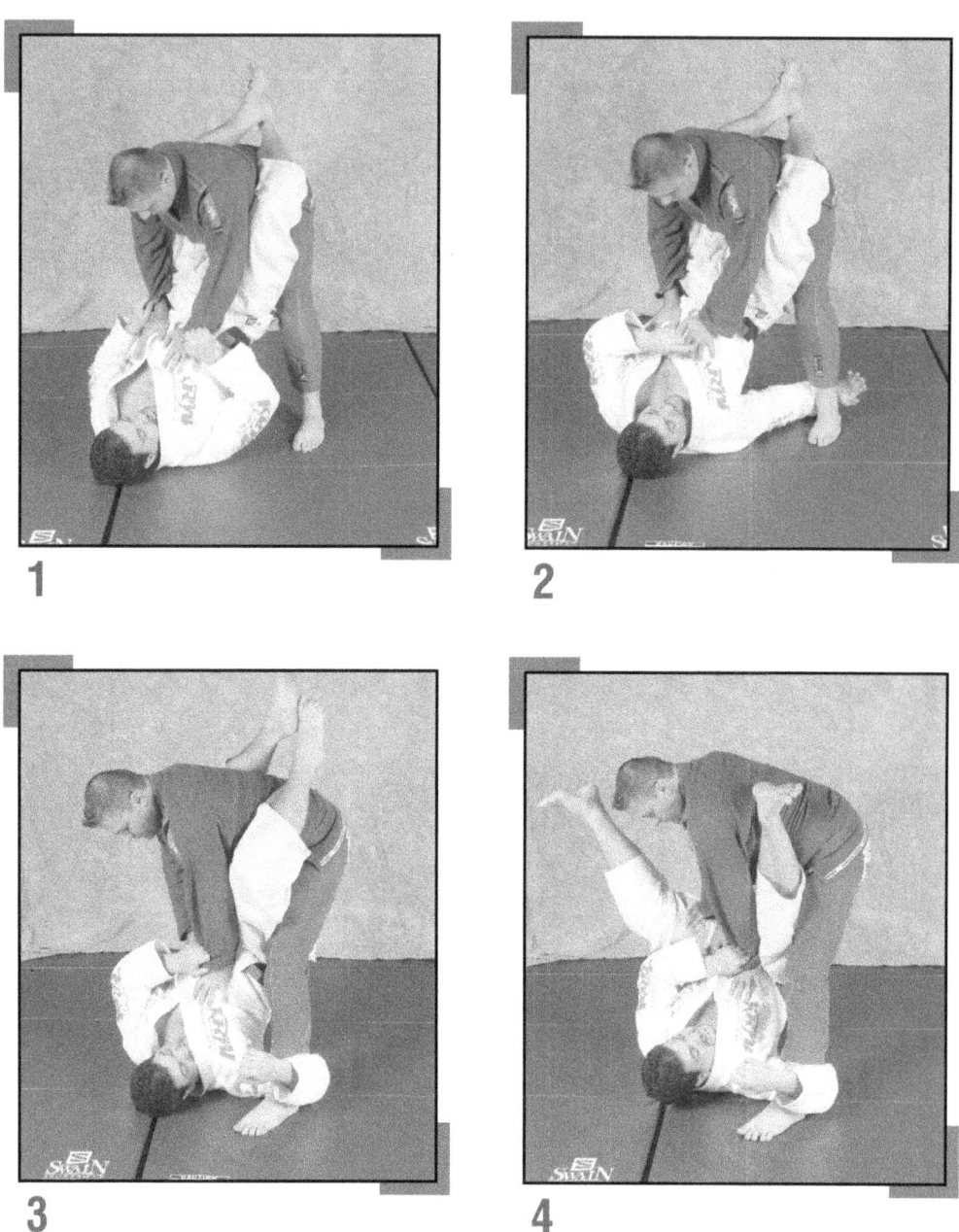

Rigan has the standing opponent inside the closed guard (1). Without opening the guard, Rigan reaches out with his right hand, grabs the opponent's left ankle (2), and brings the right arm all the way around the ankle (3), as he simultaneously opens the legs and pivots his body to the right (4).

TECHNIQUE 40

5

6

7

Then, Rigan passes his left leg all the way to the right side of the opponent's left leg **(5)**, puts pressure with his right thigh so the opponent can't get out **(6)**, and bring him down to the ground, where he applies a painful lock to the opponent's knee **(7)**.

ATTACKS FROM THE GROUND

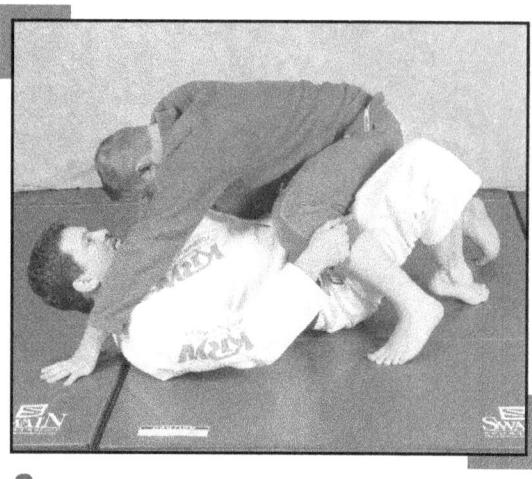

Rigan has both of his feet inside the opponent's thigh in a butterfly guard (1). Rigan uses his right hand to grab the left side of the opponent's pants and pull it toward him (2). Then, he slides his body under the opponent's and pushes the right leg all the way inside (3).

TECHNIQUE 41

4

5

6

Now, Rigan brings his right leg to the outside (4) and over the opponent's left leg without releasing the control of the foot by his right arm (5). From that position, Rigan secures the opponent's foot position and put downward pressure with his right leg to apply a footlock to the opponent's left foot (6).

ATTACKS FROM THE GROUND

1

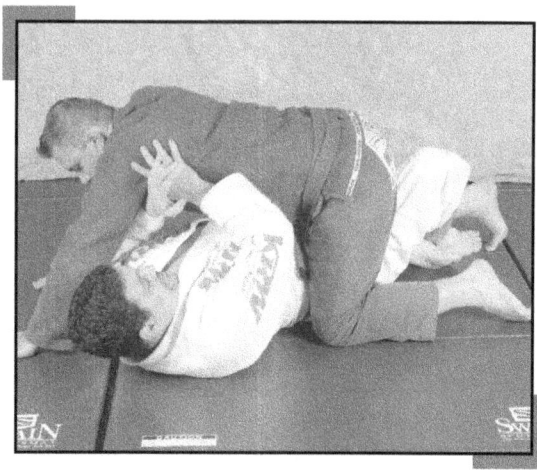
2

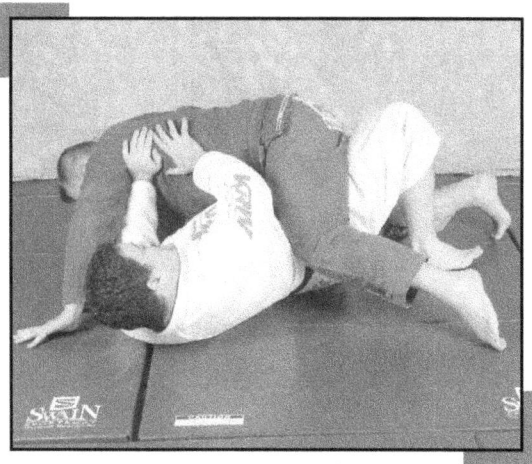
3

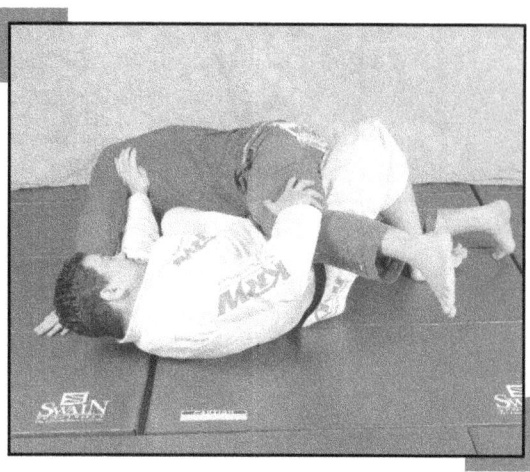
4

Rigan has the opponent under control inside of the half guard (1). Rigan uses his right hand to push the opponent's body to the left (2), to create space so he can lift his right hip (3), and control the opponent's left leg (4).

TECHNIQUE 42

5

6

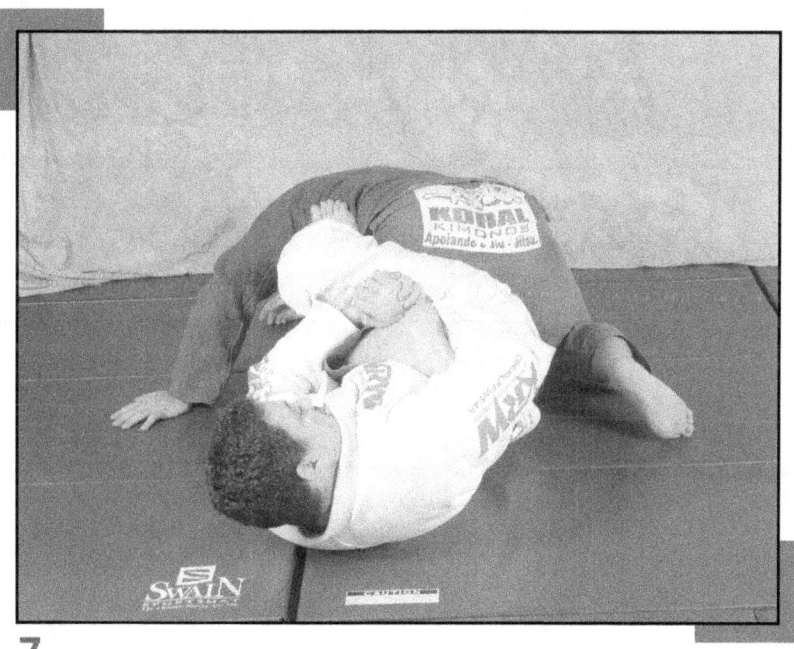
7

Once the opponent has been put out of balance and is on the opposite side of Rigan's head, Rigan brings his right leg over the opponent's left leg **(5)**, wraps his right arm around the opponent's left ankle **(6)**, and applies a devastating anklelock to the foot **(7)**.

ATTACKS FROM THE GROUND

The opponent is trying to take the back of Rigan, who is on his all-fours (1). Rigan begins the attack by raising his left knee off the floor (2). Then, he reaches with his right hand under his body (3), and grabs the opponent's left leg at the level of the thigh (4).

1

2

3

4

TECHNIQUE 43

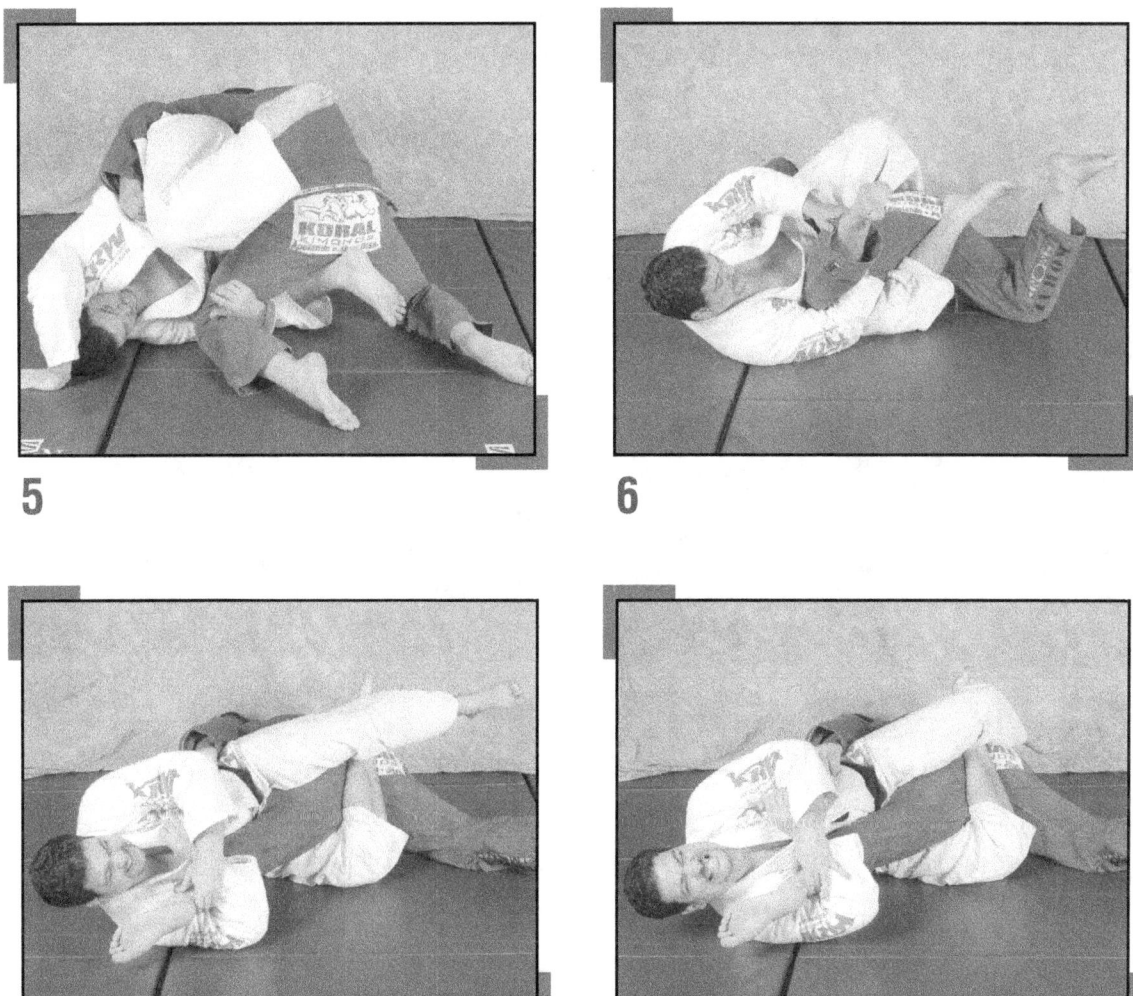

Rigan brings his head down and begins to roll forward as he uses his hips to unbalance the opponent during the sweeping action (5). Once the opponent is on the ground, Rigan controls the opponent's left leg (6), grabs the foot with both hands (7) and, straightening his body and locking his right instep under the back of his left knee, applies a painful knee-bar (8).

ATTACKS FROM THE GROUND

Rigan faces his opponent from a seated position (1). Rigan brings his left leg inside the opponent's legs (2) and leans forward as he reaches out to grab the inside of the opponent's pants (3). Then, he puts his left shoulder on the ground and properly secures the grip (4).

1

2

3

4

TECHNIQUE 44

5

6

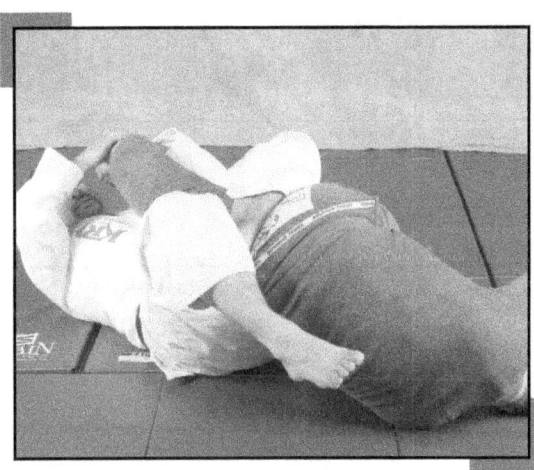
7

8

Once the grips and the positions have been secured and established, Rigan rolls forward over his left shoulder (5) and lands on the right side of the opponent's body (6). Controlling the opponent's right leg with both of his hands, he applies a painful kneebar (7). Close-up (8).

ATTACKS FROM THE GROUND

Rigan, seated, is facing the opponent, who is trying to pass the butterfly guard (1). Rigan moves his body to the right and reaches over the opponent's back to grab the belt as he simultaneously hooks his left foot under the opponent's left thigh (2). Once the opponent's body is on Rigan's left side (3), Rigan grabs the opponent's pants with his left hand (4).

1

2

3

4

TECHNIQUE 45

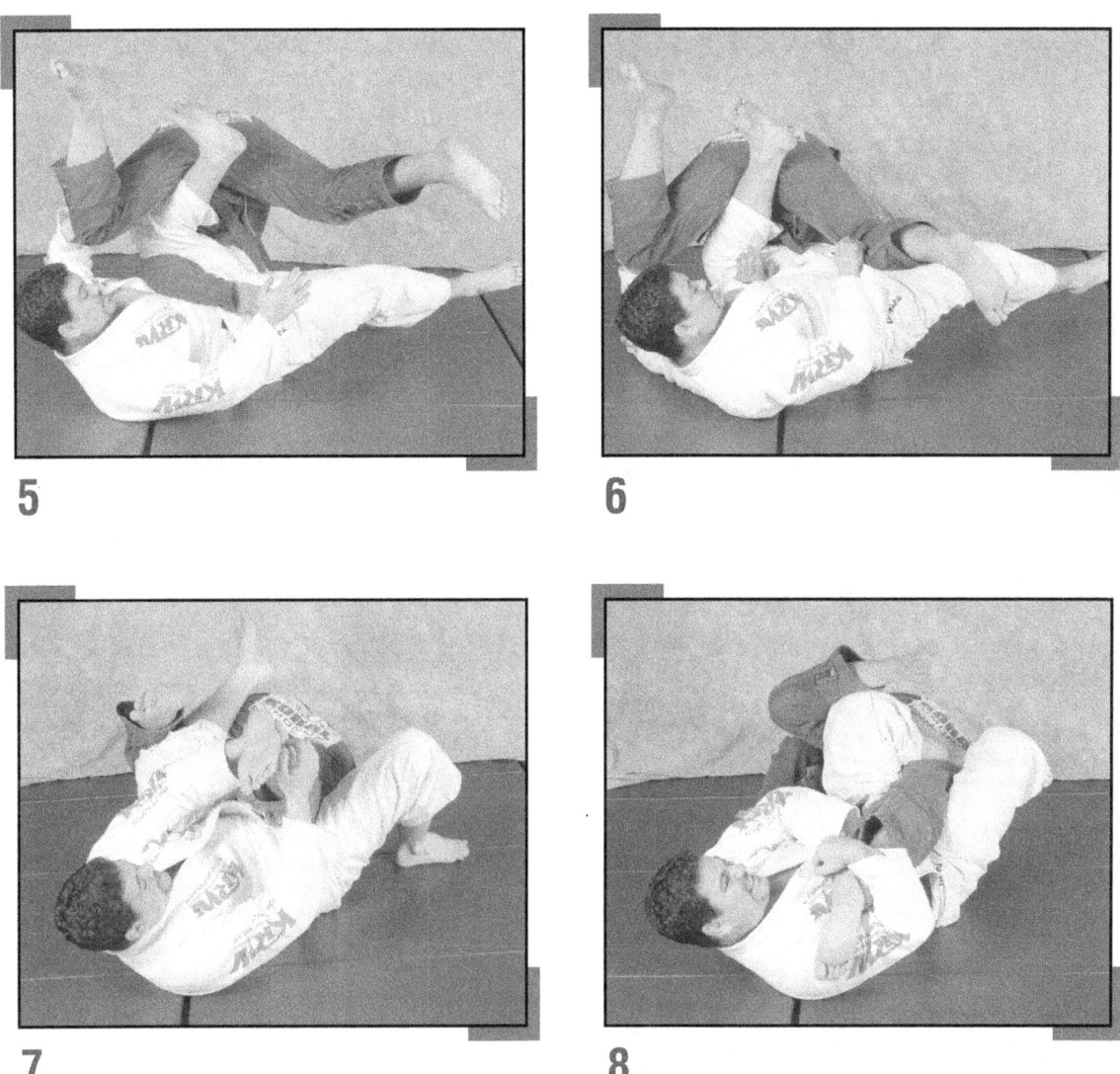

Then, he sweeps the opponent to the left by pulling with his left hand and lifting the opponent's left leg with the hook of his left foot **(5)**. When the opponent touches the ground with his body **(6)**, Rigan controls the momentum and grabs the opponent's right leg **(7)**. By pulling toward his chest with both hands and tilting his hips up, Rigan applies a knee-bar **(8)**.

ATTACKS FROM THE GROUND

Rigan has the opponent controlled in his half guard (1). Carefully, Rigan moves his body to the left as he pushes the opponent to the opposite side (2), creating space to bring the rest of his body from under the opponent (3) while, at the same time, controlling the opponent's left leg with a double leg trap (4).

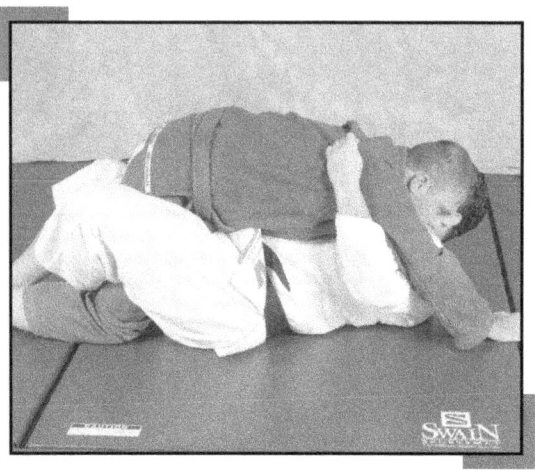

1

2

3

4

TECHNIQUE 46

5

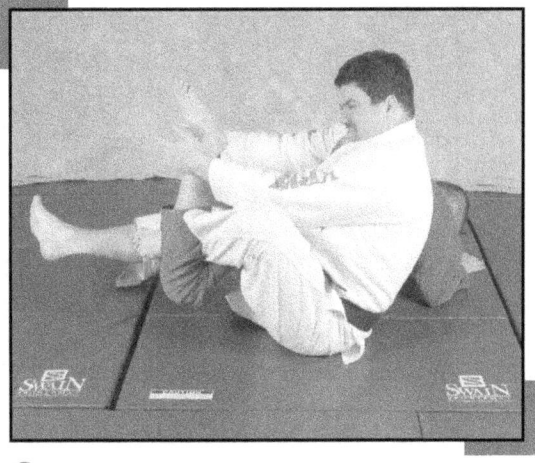
6

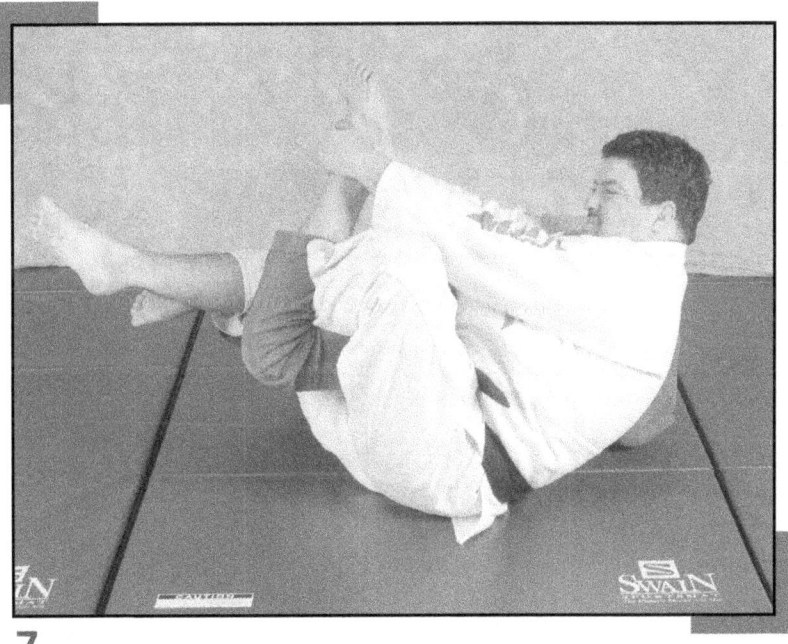
7

Rigan brings his body to the upward position (5) and, using his foot, brings the opponent's right foot closer so he can grab it with both hands (6). Then, he leans back and, creating a figure-4 control with his legs, applies a painful shin/footlock to his opponent (7).

ATTACKS FROM THE GROUND

Rigan is being attacked from behind, with the opponent applying the hooks (1). The opponent brings his left foot over the right foot, thinking that this will secure better the leg trap on Rigan's body (2). Now, Rigan pushes the opponent's feet down (3).

1

2

3

TECHNIQUE 47

4

5

6

Then, he brings his own right foot and places it on the top of both of the opponent's, trapping them **(4)**. Immediately, he places his right foot under the back of the left knee to secure the feet position **(5)** and, leaning back, puts pressure with his hips to apply a painful lock to the opponent's feet **(6)**.

ATTACKS FROM THE GROUND

The opponent, situated on Rigan's back, is controlling both of Rigan's lapels (1). Rigan brings his left hand to the outside and grabs the opponent's pants so he can place his left leg over the opponent's (2). Then, he slides his hips and brings the right foot (3) under the opponent's left leg (4).

TECHNIQUE 48

5

6

7

Rigan leans back to his right side and pulls the opponent's left leg closer to his body (5). Then, he squeezes with both legs to trap the opponent's left leg (6), and applies a finishing knee-bar (7).

ATTACKS FROM THE GROUND

The opponent is controlling Rigan on a north-south position **(1)**. Rigan pushes the opponent's trunk away with both arms **(2)**, and brings his legs up to create momentum **(3)** to unbalance the opponent and bring him to the front **(4)**.

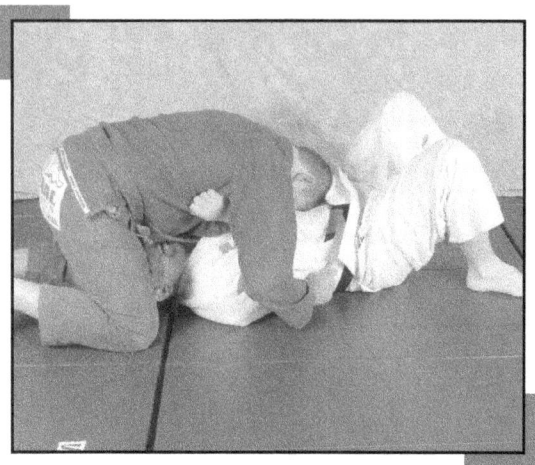

1

2

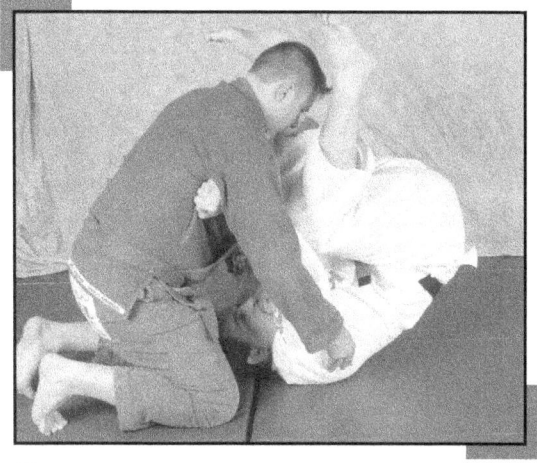

3

4

TECHNIQUE 49

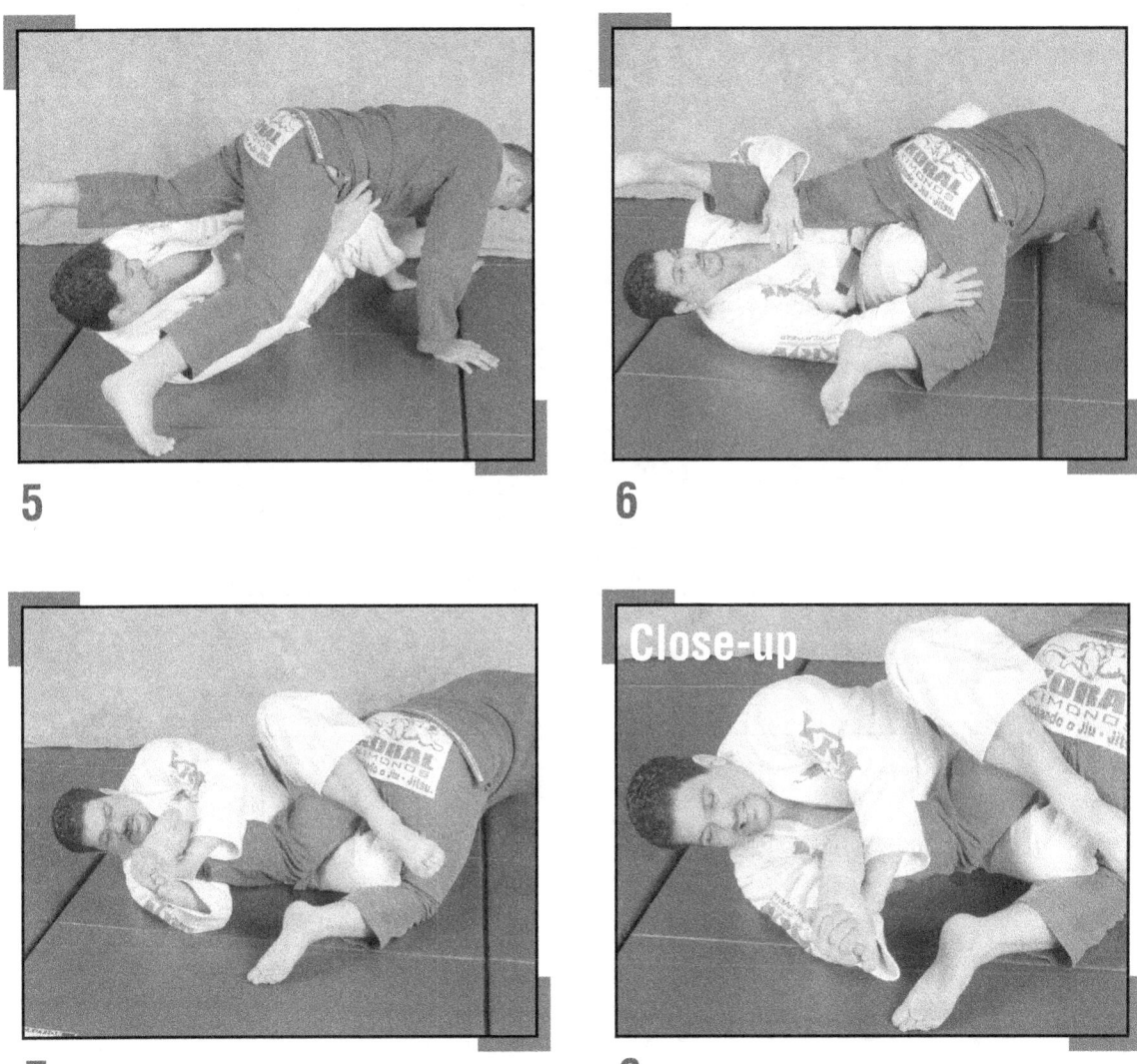

Then, he uses both legs to push the opponent a little more to the front (5), but as he allows the opponent's body to pass over him, Rigan controls the opponent's left leg with his left arm (6). Then, he secures the opponent's left leg with both hands and applies a painful lock to the opponent's foot (7). Close-up (8).

ATTACKS FROM THE GROUND

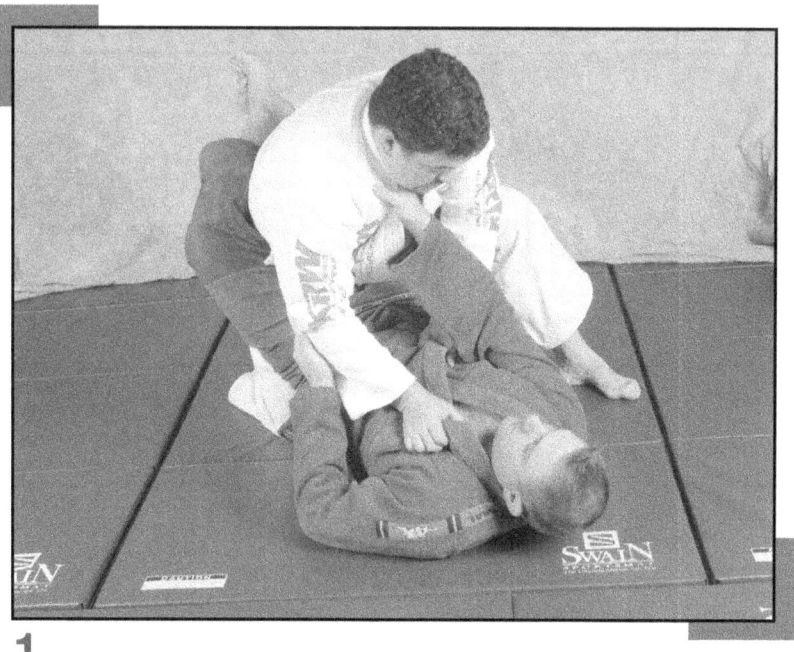

Rigan is trying to pass the opponent's guard (1) but the opponent feels the attempt (2), and begins to slide his body to the left side (3).

TECHNIQUE 50

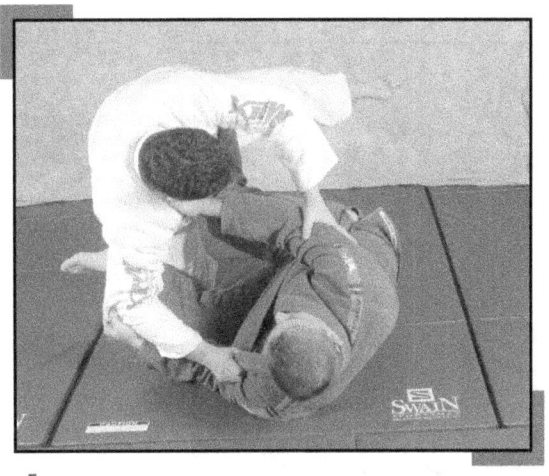
4

5

6

Then, he applies a clean sweep **(4)** by pulling with his left hand from Rigan's right sleeve and, by sweeping with his right leg, Rigan's left hip **(5)**. When the opponent is trying to get up to follow the action, Rigan stops the opponent's action by using his right hand **(6)**.

(continued on next page)

ATTACKS FROM THE GROUND

(continued from previous page)

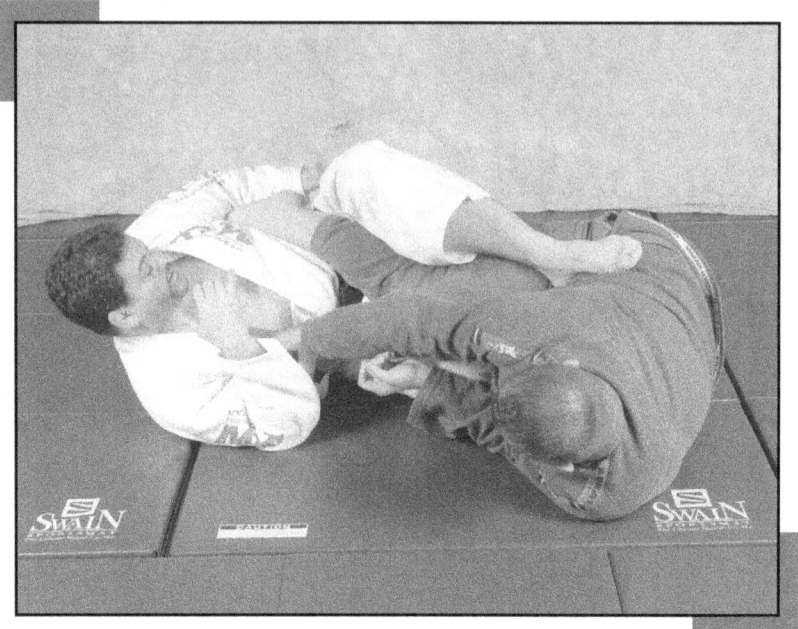

7

8

TECHNIQUE 50

9

Then, he brings his left leg over the opponent's right (7), secures the foot under his left armpit (8), and applies a reverse footlock (9).

ATTACKS FROM THE GROUND

Rigan is mounted on the opponent's stomach (1). Then, he brings his right foot up (2), and puts it inside of the opponent's left thigh (3). This action creates space and momentum so he can pass his left leg all the way to the opposite side of the opponent's body (4).

1

2

3

4

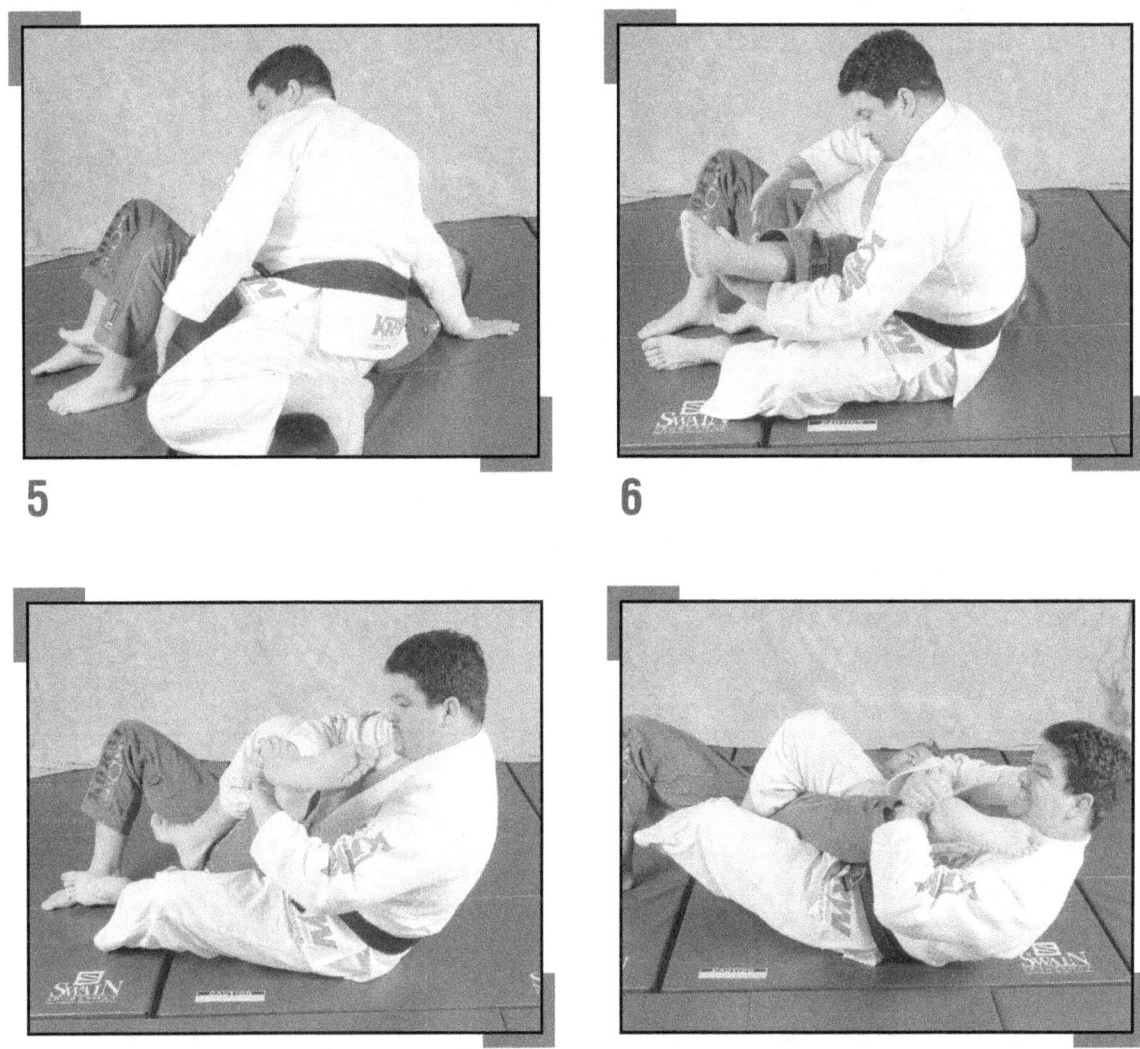

Without bringing his right leg from inside of the opponent's (5), Rigan reaches for the opponent's left foot with both hands (6), and pulls back as he allows his body to fall into the ground (7) to apply a knee-bar (8).

ATTACKS FROM THE GROUND

1

2

3

Rigan controls the opponent from the mount position (1). The opponent, trying to escape, moves his body to the right to create space on the left side (2) so he can push Rigan's right knee and use the hip escape (3).

TECHNIQUE 52

4

5

6

Rigan feels the escape attempt and immediately brings his right knee to the ground, which forces the opponent to lock his legs to prevent Rigan from mounting him again **(4)**. Then, Rigan moves his body to the left side **(5)**, and traps the opponent's right leg **(6)**.

(continued on next page)

ATTACKS FROM THE GROUND

(continued from previous page)

7

8

TECHNIQUE 52

9

Without releasing control of the leg, Rigan rolls to his left side (7) and grabs the opponent's trapped leg with his right hand (8), to apply a figure-4 leglock to the opponent's shin/foot (9).

ATTACKS FROM THE STANDING POSITION

- Technique 1 144
- Technique 2 146
- Technique 3 150
- Technique 4 154
- Technique 5 158
- Technique 6 160
- Technique 7 164
- Technique 8 168
- Technique 9 172
- Technique 10 176
- Technique 11 180
- Technique 12 182
- Technique 13 184
- Technique 14 186
- Technique 15 188
- Technique 16 192
- Technique 17 194
- Technique 18 198
- Technique 19 202

ATTACKS FROM THE STANDING POSITION

1

2

3

Rigan faces his opponent (1). He brings his left leg in front of the opponent's right leg (2) and then puts it across both thighs without releasing the grips on the collar and the left sleeve of the opponent's gi (3).

Encyclopedia of Leglocks

TECHNIQUE 1

4

5

6

7

Rigan brings his left leg behind the opponent **(4)** and, with a scissors takedown, brings him to the ground **(5)**. Without losing control of the right leg, Rigan uses his right hand to pull the opponent's leg close to his body **(6)** and applies a knee-bar secured by doing a lock with both of his legs in a figure-4 trap **(7)**.

ATTACKS FROM THE STANDING POSITION

Rigan faces his opponent (1). He brings his left leg in front of the opponent's right leg (2) and then puts it across both thighs, and uses his right hand to control his own body movement (3).

TECHNIQUE 2

4

5

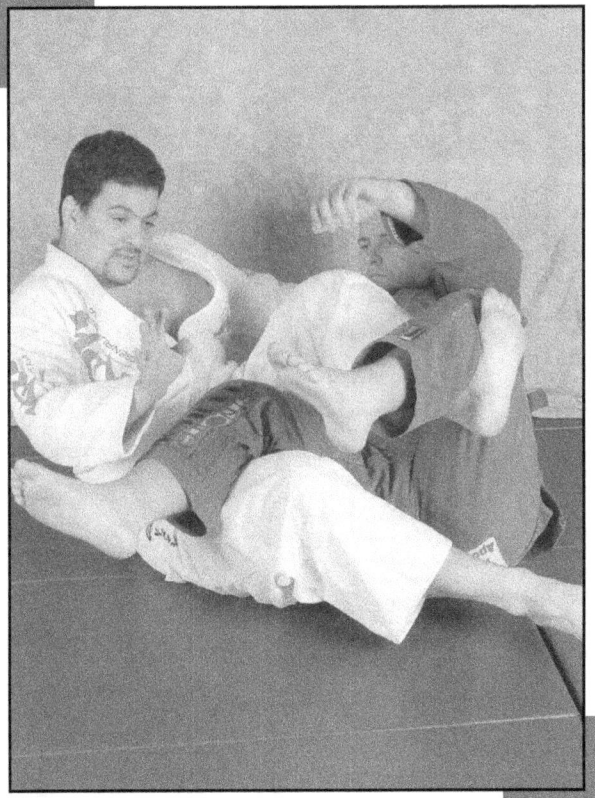

6

Rigan brings his left leg behind the opponent (4) and, with a scissors takedown, brings him to the ground (5). This time, he uses his left foot to hook the opponent's left leg (6).

(continued on next page)

ATTACKS FROM THE STANDING POSITION

(continued from previous page)

7

8

9

10

TECHNIQUE 2

Close-up

11

He brings it close to him and grabs his with his right hand **(7)**, putting it close to the right leg **(8)**. Then, he passes his right arm around, wrapping both feet **(9)** with the left foot over the right, to apply a double footlock **(10)**. Close-up **(11)**.

ATTACKS FROM THE STANDING POSITION

1

2

3

Rigan faces his opponent (1). He brings his left leg in front of the opponent's right leg (2), and then he tries to put it across both legs, but the opponent moves his left leg to the outside and prevents this action from happening (3).

TECHNIQUE 3

4

5

6

Rigan sees the impossibility of applying a scissors takedown with both legs and reaches with his right hand **(4)** to grab the opponent's left ankle **(5)**. Then, he pulls back and simultaneously pushes with the left side of his body to unbalance the opponent **(6)**.

(continued on next page)

ATTACKS FROM THE STANDING POSITION

(continued from previous page)

This movement brings the opponent to the ground (7). Rigan doesn't lose control of the opponent's left leg and begins to secure the position by bringing his left knee closer to the opponent's stomach (8).

7

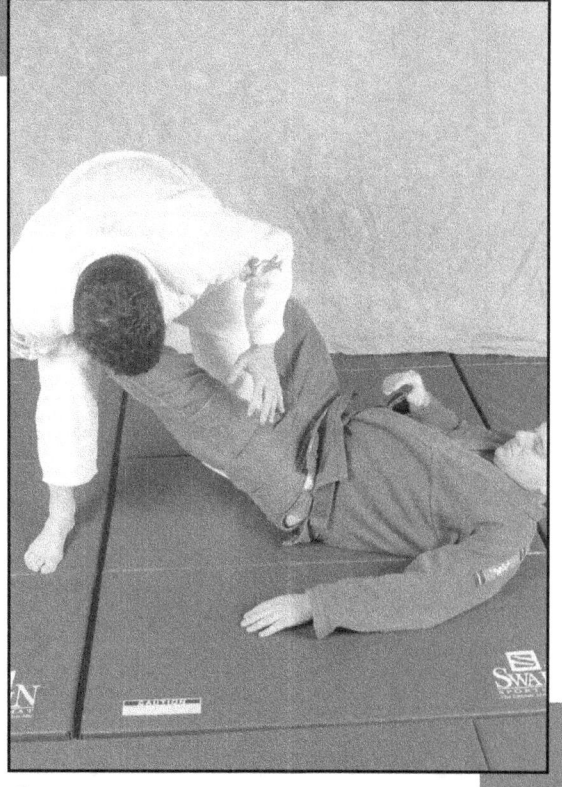

8

TECHNIQUE 3

9

Then, with his right hand, he wraps the opponent's left ankle around, puts more pressure on the opponent's stomach with his left knee, and applies a painful footlock (9).

ATTACKS FROM THE STANDING POSITION

1

2

3

Rigan faces his opponent (1). He brings his left leg in front of the opponent's right leg (2) and then brings the left leg back to apply a throw (3).

TECHNIQUE 4

The opponent blocks this action by grabbing Rigan from the back **(4)**, which makes Rigan lose his balance **(5)**. Rigan then rolls forward to break the opponent's advantageous position **(6)**.

(continued on next page)

ATTACKS FROM THE STANDING POSITION

(continued from previous page)

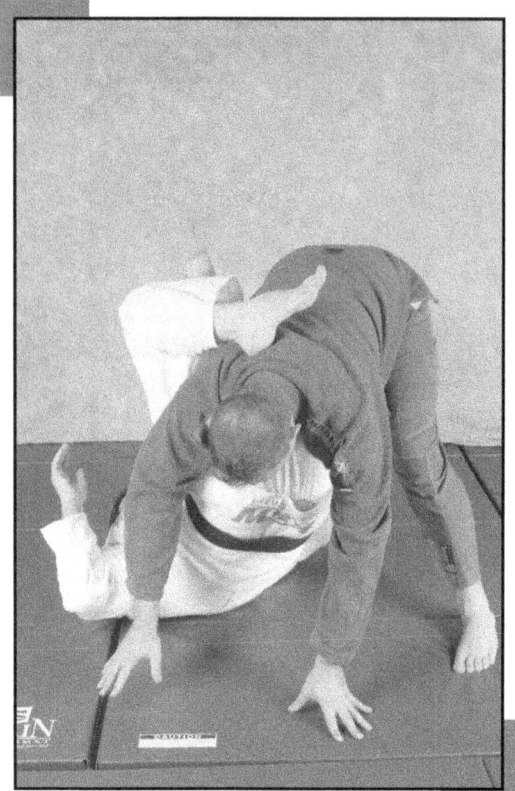

7

By using his right leg for added leverage **(7)**, Rigan pushes the opponent to the ground **(8)** and, after securing the opponent's right leg with both hands, he applies a knee-bar **(9)**.

8

9

ATTACKS FROM THE STANDING POSITION

1

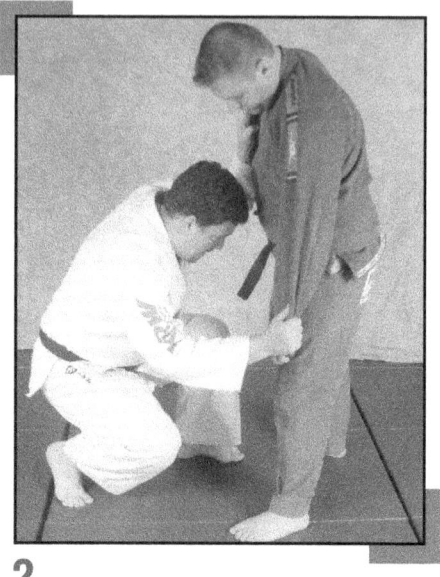

2

Rigan faces his opponent with an orthodox collar/sleeve grip (1). Rigan drops his body (2) and sits on the ground and inside the opponent's legs, with the right leg straight and the left leg placed inside the opponent's right thigh (3).

3

TECHNIQUE 5

4

5

6

From his back, Rigan maintains control of the opponent's left sleeve, and brings his right leg from the outside in a wrapping motion over the opponent's left leg (4). Then, he pushes the opponent's right thigh with his left leg as he simultaneously wraps the opponent's left ankle with the right arm (5). Once the proper control has been applied, Rigan adds pressure for a painful lock to the ankle (6).

ATTACKS FROM THE STANDING POSITION

Rigan faces his opponent with an orthodox collar/sleeve grip (1). Rigan pulls with the right hand to bring the opponent closer (2) so he can switch the grip and grab the opponent's pants at the knee level (3).

TECHNIQUE 6

4

5

6

Then, he pulls hard to create space **(4)**, to put his left leg between the opponent's **(5)**, to sweep the right leg and throw him onto the ground **(6)**.

(continued on next page)

ATTACKS FROM THE STANDING POSITION

(continued from previous page)

7

8

9

Once on the ground, Rigan controls the opponent's body with his left hand and the opponent's right leg with his right hand (7). Then, he brings his right hand around the opponent's right ankle (8) and secures the grip with his left hand placed on the opponent's shin for better leverage (9).

TECHNIQUE 6

10

Then, Rigan applies pressure and lifts his body to apply a painful footlock (10).

ATTACKS FROM THE STANDING POSITION

Rigan faces his opponent, who is using the open guard (1). Rigan passes his right hand under the opponent's left leg as he simultaneously secures the right leg with his left hand (2). Then, he pushes the opponent's left leg to the side (3).

TECHNIQUE 7

4

5

6

By creating space with the last action, Rigan now can bring his right foot close to the opponent's left hip (4). Then, he turns around as he simultaneously maintains control of the opponent's left leg (5), and begins to drop his body to the ground (6).

(continued on next page)

ATTACKS FROM THE STANDING POSITION

(continued from previous page)

7

8

TECHNIQUE 7

9

Once on the ground, Rigan secures the opponent's body position by using both of his legs as, at the same time, he grabs the opponent's left leg **(7)**. He pulls hard with both hands and, with his left foot, pushes the opponent's right leg **(8)**. Then, he brings his right leg over the opponent's left leg, puts his right instep under the back of his left leg to secure the position, and applies a knee-bar to the opponent's left leg **(9)**.

ATTACKS FROM THE STANDING POSITION

Rigan faces his opponent with an orthodox collar/sleeve grip (1). Rigan moves his left foot to the outside of the opponent's position (2), and brings his right knee up (3).

TECHNIQUE 8

4

5

6

Then, he brings it down behind the opponent's right leg (4), to apply a leg throw (5) by pulling the opponent's right sleeve with the left hand and by pushing the opponent's left collar with the right hand (6).

(continued on next page)

ATTACKS FROM THE STANDING POSITION

(continued from previous page)

7

8

9

With the opponent on the ground **(7)**, Rigan brings his right knee up to control the opponent's right leg, without releasing the grip on the left collar **(8)**. Then, he switches grips and allows his left hand to control the opponent's right knee as he simultaneously begins to bring his right hand back **(9)**.

TECHNIQUE 8

10

Then, he squeezes hard with both legs to trap the opponent's right leg, and passes his right arm behind the opponent's ankle (10).

He closes the grip by using his left hand, and applies a painful anklelock to the opponent (11).

11

ATTACKS FROM THE STANDING POSITION

1

2

Rigan faces his opponent with an orthodox collar/sleeve grip (1). Rigan moves his left foot to the outside of the opponent's position (2) and brings his right knee up (3).

3

TECHNIQUE 9

4

5

6

Then, he brings it down behind the opponent's right leg (4), to apply a leg throw (5) by pulling the opponent's right sleeve with the left hand and by pushing the opponent's left collar with the right hand (6).

(continued on next page)

ATTACKS FROM THE STANDING POSITION

(continued from previous page)

7

8

9

With the opponent on the ground (7), Rigan brings his right knee up to control the opponent's right leg without releasing the grip on the left collar (8). Then, he switches grips and allows his left hand to control the opponent's left hip as he simultaneously begins to bring his right hand back (9).

TECHNIQUE 9

10

11

12

Now, Rigan brings his left knee around the opponent's left side of the groin **(10)**, and sits down next to his body as he controls the opponent's right leg with his right hand **(11)**. Rigan leans back, puts his right foot over the opponent's left thigh for better control, and applies a knee-bar **(12)**.

ATTACKS FROM THE STANDING POSITION

Rigan is facing his opponent with an orthodox collar/sleeve grip (1). Rigan drops his body (2), and grabs the opponent left ankle with his right hand (3).

TECHNIQUE 10

4

5

6

Once he has secured the grip on the opponent's foot **(4)**, Rigan stands up and pulls back on the ankle as he simultaneously pushes with his left hand **(5)**. He brings his body all the way up and wraps the opponent's left leg with his right hand **(6)**.

(continued on next page)

ATTACKS FROM THE STANDING POSITION

(continued from previous page)

Rigan uses his left leg to push the opponent's right leg away **(7)**, which forces the opponent to go to the ground. Rigan doesn't lose control of the opponent's left leg when he falls on the ground **(8)**.

TECHNIQUE 10

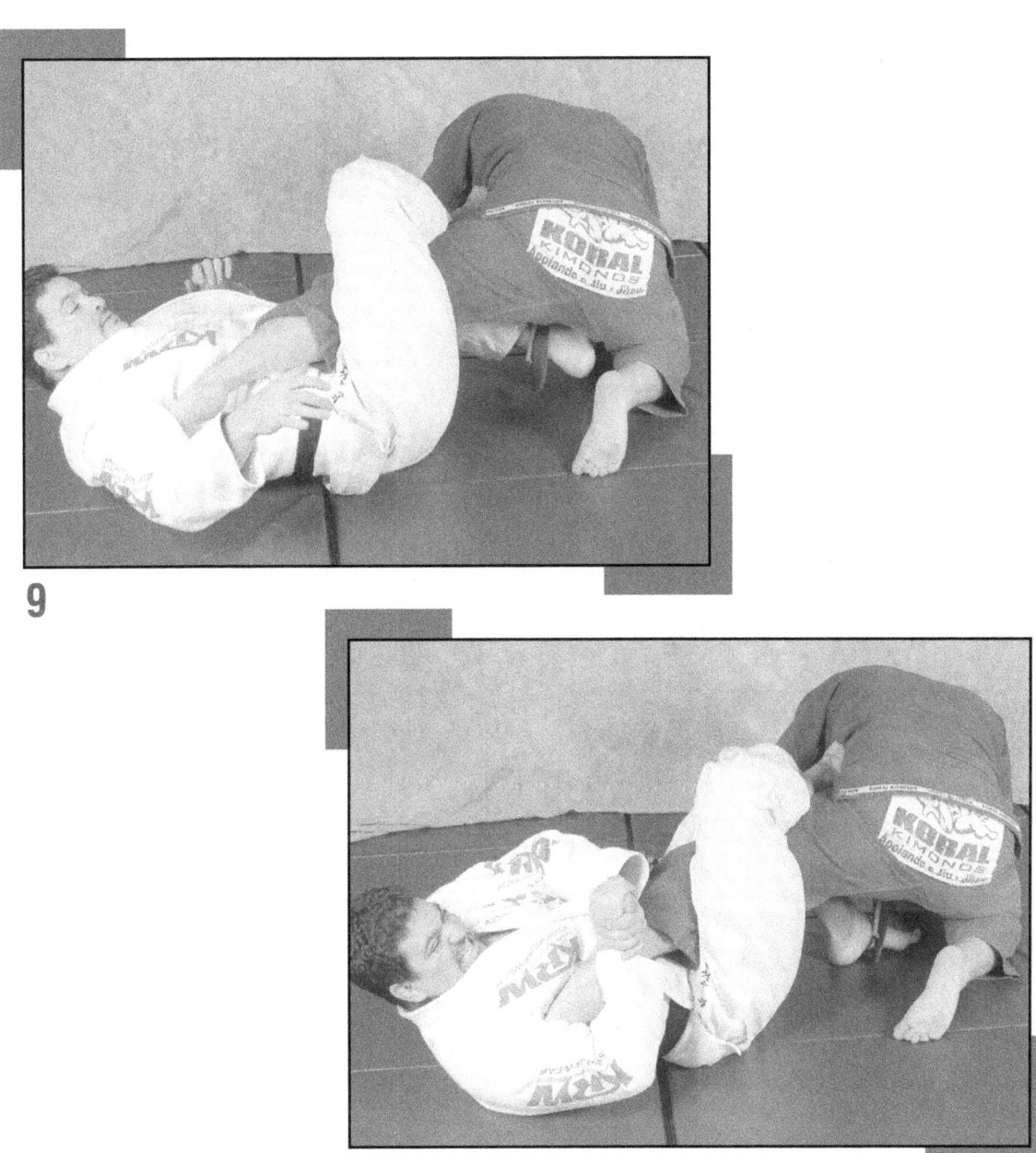

Then, he passes his right leg over the opponent's left leg **(9)**, and applies a reverse anklelock **(10)**.

ATTACKS FROM THE STANDING POSITION

1

2

3

Rigan, standing, faces his opponent, who is using the open guard (1). Rigan uses his left hand to control the opponent's body as he simultaneously brings his right hand to the side to grab the opponent's pants (2). Then, he leans back and sits on the ground as he traps the opponent's left foot under the armpit (3).

TECHNIQUE 11

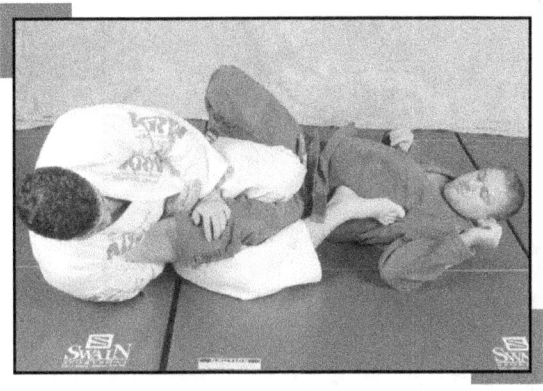
4

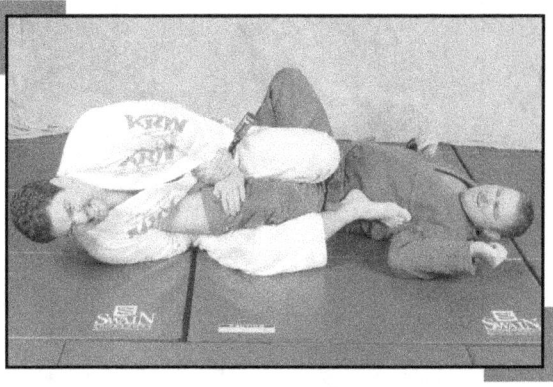
5

6

Rigan secures the grip, using his left hand to control the opponent's left shin **(4)**. Then, he squeezes both thighs to maintain the opponent's leg in place **(5)**, and applies a painful footlock **(6)**.

ATTACKS FROM THE STANDING POSITION

1

2

3

Rigan, standing, faces his opponent, who is using the open guard (1). He passes his right hand around the opponent's left leg (2), and wraps the ankle with his right arm as he simultaneously secures the opponent's body with his left hand (3).

TECHNIQUE 12

4

Rigan brings his left hand to the front and places it on the opponent's left shin as he secures the grip **(4)**.

Then, he puts pressure with his left knee on the opponent's body and brings his right knee close to the opponent's left leg to apply a footlock from the standing position **(5)**.

5

ATTACKS FROM THE STANDING POSITION

1

2

3

4

Rigan, standing, faces his opponent, who is using the open guard (1). He passes his right hand around the opponent's left leg (2), and wraps the ankle with his right arm as he simultaneously secures the opponent's body with his left hand (3). Then, he leans back and sits on the ground as he traps the opponent's left foot under the armpit (4).

TECHNIQUE 13

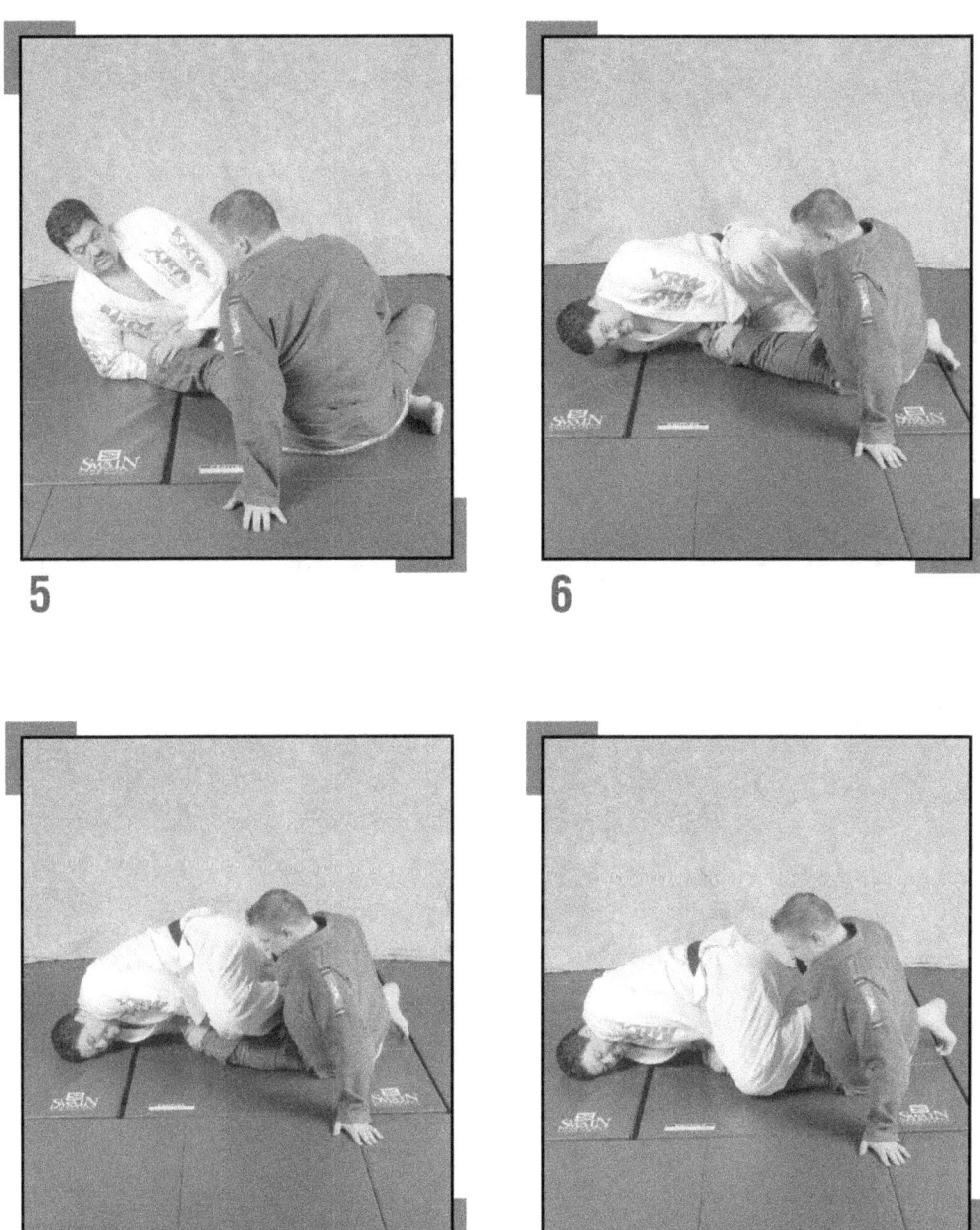

Rigan secures the grip, using his left hand to control the opponent's left shin (5). Then, he brings his left leg over the opponent's right leg (6), squeezes both thighs to maintain the opponent's leg in place (7), and applies a painful footlock (8).

ATTACKS FROM THE STANDING POSITION

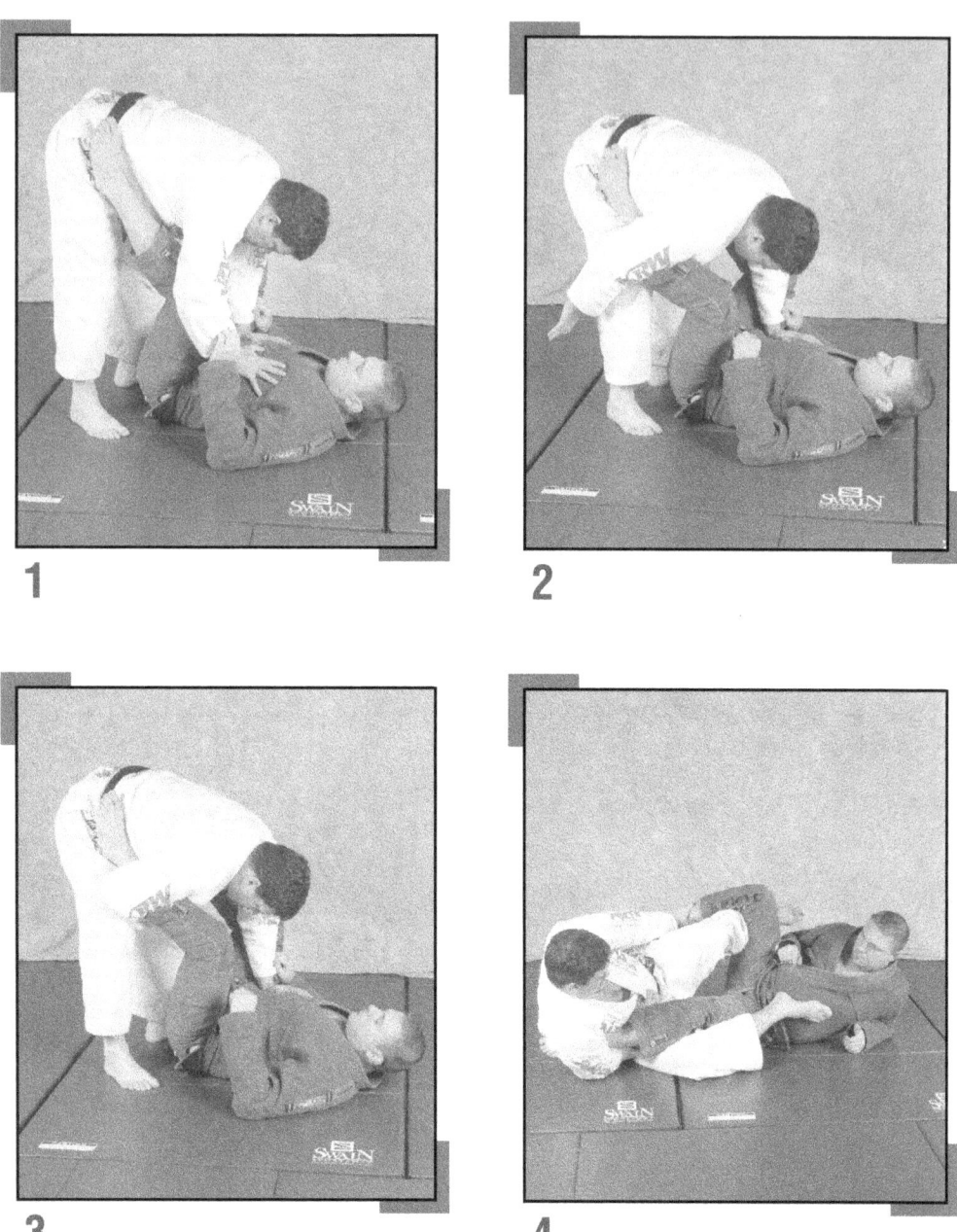

Rigan, standing, faces his opponent, who is using the open guard (1). He passes his right hand around the opponent's left leg (2) and wraps the ankle with his right arm as he simultaneously secures the opponent's body with his left hand (3). Then, he leans back and sits on the ground as he traps the opponent's left foot under the armpit. Rigan uses his left leg to control the opponent's attempt to stand up (4).

TECHNIQUE 14

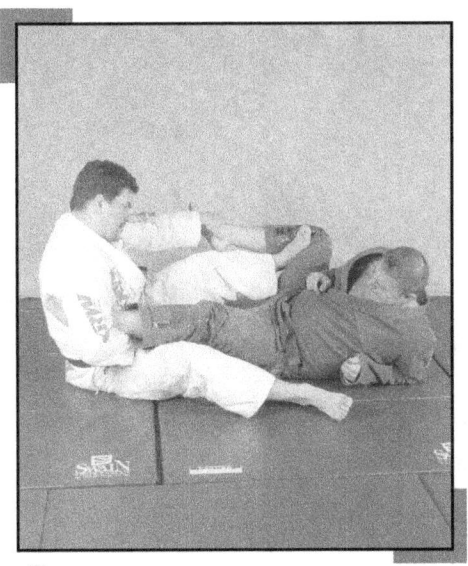

5

6

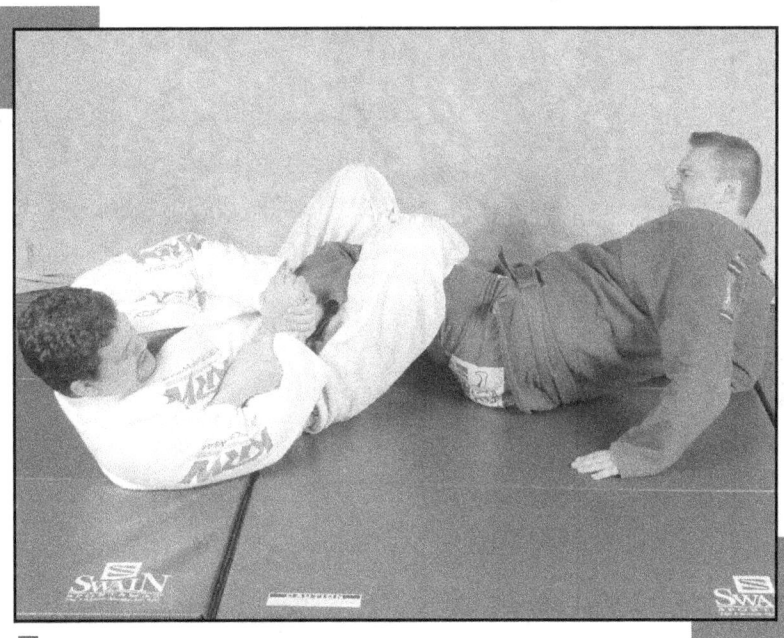

7

Holding the opponent's right leg with his left hand, Rigan pushes it away, using his left foot (5). Then, he brings the right leg over the opponent's left thigh (6), and applies an anklelock to the opponent's left foot (7).

ATTACKS FROM THE STANDING POSITION

Rigan faces his opponent (1). He brings his hips down before initiating the attack (2).

TECHNIQUE 15

3

4

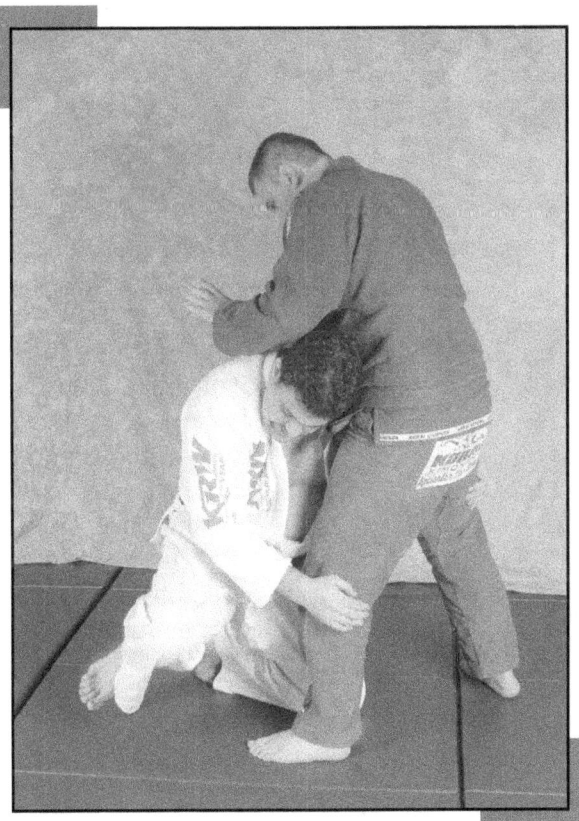
5

With his center of gravity low (3), Rigan closes the distance and grabs the opponent's legs with both hands (4). Then, he brings his right knee forward and keeps his head close to the opponent's body (5).

(continued on next page)

ATTACKS FROM THE STANDING POSITION

(continued from previous page)

Rigan brings his right foot to the side (6) and places it right behind the opponent's left leg (7). Then, he traps the opponent's left ankle with his right foot (8) and takes the opponent down to the ground without losing the control of the left leg (9). Rigan locks the opponent's leg, using his two legs and, straightening his body, applies a painful knee-bar (10).

TECHNIQUE 15

9

10

ATTACKS FROM THE STANDING POSITION

1

2

3

Rigan, standing, faces his opponent, who is using the open guard (1). Rigan moves his body forward and put pressure on the opponent's guard (2). The opponent can't keep Rigan away and tries to roll with the push (3).

TECHNIQUE 16

4

5

6

Rigan keeps pushing forward (4), and ends up turning the opponent around (5). Then, he maintains control of the opponent's left leg and applies a reverse anklelock (6).

ATTACKS FROM THE STANDING POSITION

1

2

3

Rigan, standing, faces his opponent, who is using the open guard (1). The opponent grabs both Rigan's ankles (2), and lift his hips to begin to unbalance Rigan's position (3).

TECHNIQUE 17

4

5

6

Then, he pulls hard with both legs and pushes away with his legs **(4–5)**, which brings Rigan to the ground. Rigan, although has been swept by the opponent's action, doesn't lose contact with the opponent's left foot that is under his right armpit **(6)**.

(continued on next page)

ATTACKS FROM THE STANDING POSITION

(continued from previous page)

7

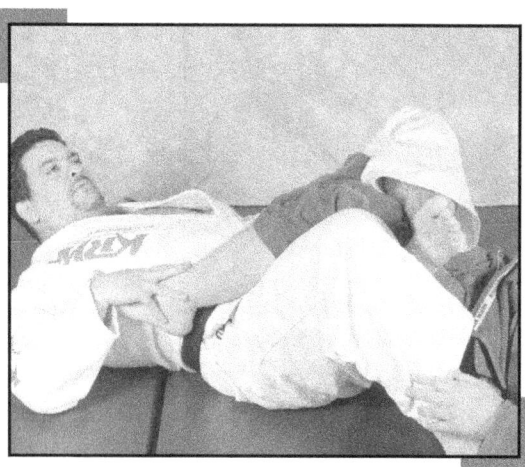
8

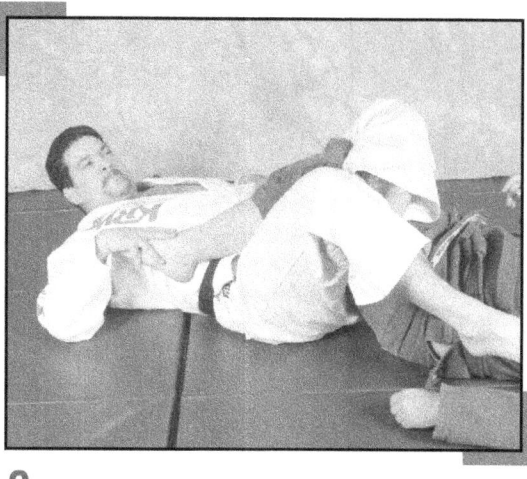
9

The opponent tries to get up and mount after applying the sweeping technique, but Rigan uses his legs to prevent the opponent's body from coming any closer **(7)**. Then, he pushes the opponent's left foot with his right hand **(8)**, controls it from the outside as he simultaneously traps the opponent's leg by doing a figure-4 lock with his own legs **(9)**.

TECHNIQUE 17

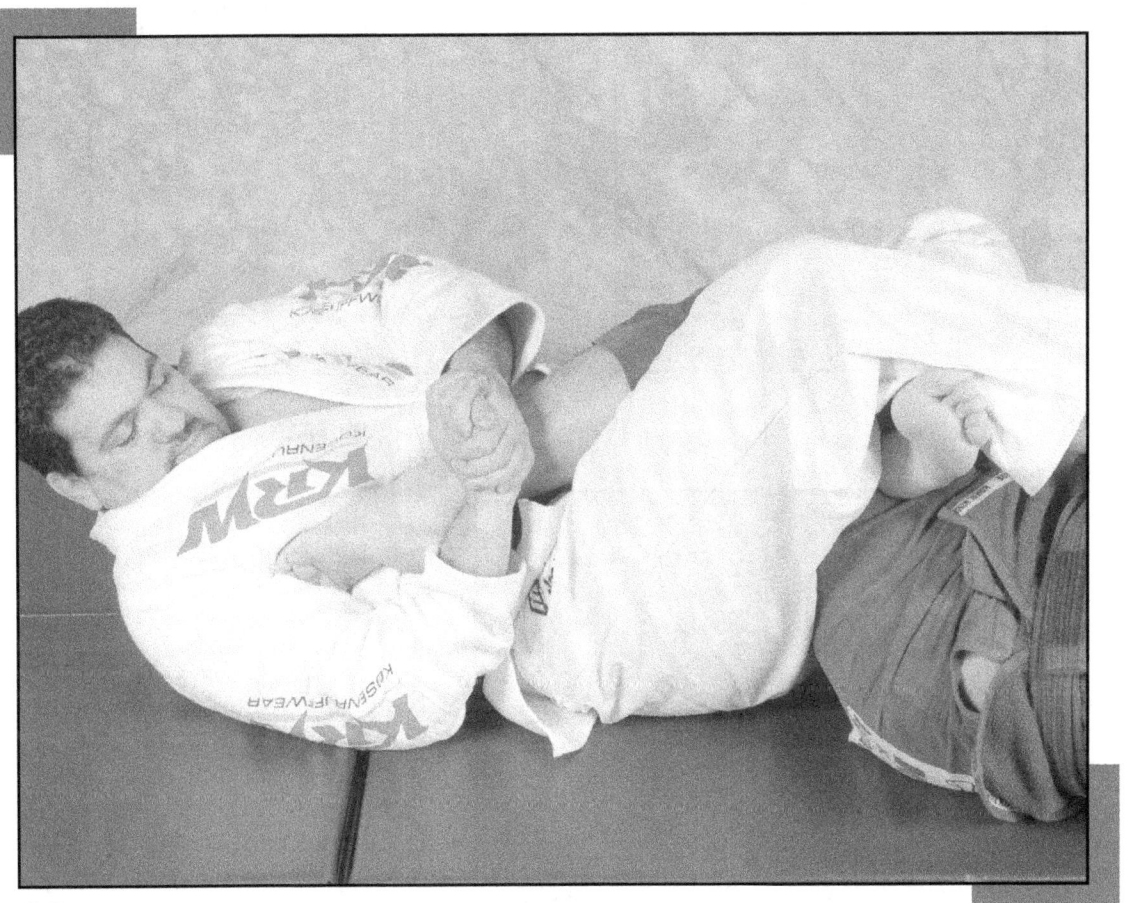

10

From a position of full control, Rigan grabs his right hand with his left, and applies a devastating anklelock, as he simultaneously twists the opponent's left knee to inflict more pain **(10)**.

ATTACKS FROM THE STANDING POSITION

1

2

3

Rigan is facing his opponent with an orthodox collar/sleeve grip (1). Rigan moves his body to the side and brings his left leg inside the opponent's (2), to hook the opponent's left leg with the instep of his left leg (3).

TECHNIQUE 18

Rigan drops his body onto the ground as he applies a scissor sweep (4),

bringing the opponent down as he maintains his left foot hooked under the opponent's left leg (5).

(continued on next page)

ATTACKS FROM THE STANDING POSITION

(continued from previous page)

6

7

From that position, Rigan uses his left hand to pull the opponent backward and totally out of balance (6). Then, he reaches for the opponent's right leg, which is trapped between his (Rigan's) own legs (7).

TECHNIQUE 18

8

9

Rigan wraps his arm around the opponent's right foot **(8)**, and applies a painful lock to the opponent's ankle **(9)**.

ATTACKS FROM THE STANDING POSITION

1

2

3

Rigan is trying to control the opponent who is sitting on the ground (1). Rigan grabs the opponent's back of the collar with his right hand as he simultaneously passes his left leg to the left side of the opponent's body (2). Then, he sits down but maintains full control of the opponent's collar (3).

TECHNIQUE 19

4

5

6

Without releasing the grip of the collar with the right hand, Rigan brings his right foot under the back of his left leg (4) and grabs the opponent's left leg with his left arm (5). Rigan leans backward and falls on the ground, from where he applies a painful kneebar as he simultaneously controls the opponent's right leg with his left foot to prevent the opponent from coming forward (6).

CONCLUSION

The use of leg-locks in BJJ, submission grappling, and MMA is a true example of how the evolution of the sport affects the development of new techniques in competition. Although the training and use of these specific techniques have existed for many years from the old Japanese Ju Jutsu and Judo to the more modern versions and styles of grappling like Sambo and Shoot Wrestling, it has been only recently that the necessity of their use has become apparent. After all, in the search for technical efficiency, there is nothing wrong in using and applying what is useful.

Finally, let us conclude this book with a few words of advice. Always remain receptive to the teachings of a qualified instructor. Study them carefully in all their details. Try these techniques out on all possible opponents, strive constantly to improve them, and you will be successful with them. One can never know too much technique.

And although everybody suffers brief periods of "staleness," try to keep them as short as possible by not forgetting that "staleness" is a mental rather than physical failing. Remember, the best way to develop any technique is through constant practice, and experience is always your best teacher.

Enjoy.

ENCYCLOPEDIA OF LEGLOCKS

NOTES

ENCYCLOPEDIA OF LEGLOCKS

NOTES

www.ingramcontent.com/pod-product-compliance
Lightning Source LLC
Chambersburg PA
CBHW081346080526
44588CB00016B/2395